W9-BED-306

Vintage Camper Trailers

Vintage Camper Trailers

Paul and Caroline Lacitinola

GIBBS SMITH
TO ENRICH AND INSPIRE HUMANKIND

This book is dedicated to the most influential women in my life: my mom, Lorry—without whom I would have never started it; and my wife, Caroline—without whom it would have never been finished.

—Paul Lacitinola

Names: Lacitinola, Paul. | Lacitinola, Caroline.
Title: Vintage camper trailers / Paul and Caroline Lacitinola.
Description: First edition. | Layton, Utah : Gibbs Smith, 2016.
Identifiers: LCCN 2015038658 | ISBN 9781423641889
Subjects: LCSH: Camping trailers--Collectors and collecting--United States.
|
   Campers (Persons)--United States--Biography.
Classification: LCC TL297 .L33 2016 | DDC 629.2260973--dc23
LC record available at http://lccn.loc.gov/2015038658 ISBN 13: 978-1-4236-4188-9

First Edition
20 19 18 17 16   5 4 3 2 1

Published by
Gibbs Smith
P.O. Box 667
Layton, Utah 84041

1.800.835.4993 orders
www.gibbs-smith.com

Designed by Kurt Wahlner
Printed and bound in Hong Kong

Gibbs Smith books are printed on either recycled, 100% post-consumer waste, FSC-certified papers or on paper produced from sustainable PEFC-certified forest/controlled wood source. Learn more at www.pefc.org.
Library of Congress Cataloging-in-Publication Data

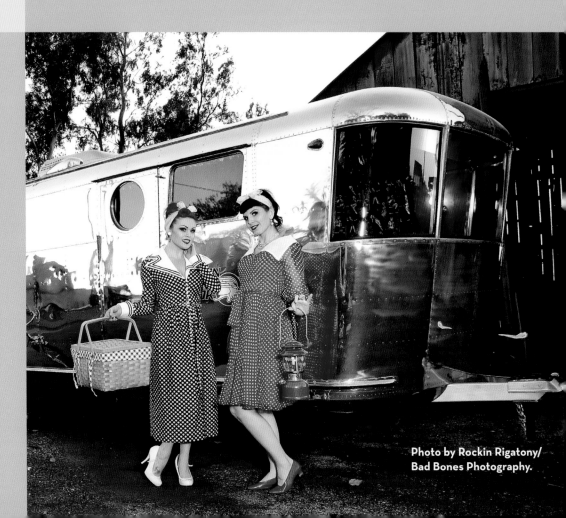

Photo by Rockin Rigatony/ Bad Bones Photography.

Contents

Preface

In 2006, we wanted to take our two kids, Angelo and Grace, camping. Tent camping seemed to pose added difficulties with two kids under three years old. Our neighbors were selling their 1962 DeVille camper trailer and we jumped at the opportunity to buy it. As owners of classic cars and motorcycles, the idea of owning something old wasn't a foreign concept to us. We were excited to go camping, but had no idea how that simple $500 trailer purchase would change our lives in such a positive way.

The Lacitinolas' 1948 Trailercraft. Photo by Clay Whiteley.

We thoroughly enjoyed camping in our little trailer. While camping, we soon realized that people had a real emotional connection with vintage trailers. We were often stopped by fellow campers as they reminisced about their time spent in trailers from a bygone era. As an old-car guy, Paul decided that the antique car world would really love vintage camper trailers and started writing a monthly article for our local car paper, *Cruisin' News*. It didn't take long for other vintage car and trailer fanatics to contact us after reading the articles. Those vintage camper trailer enthusiasts welcomed us into the hobby and introduced us to rallies on the West Coast.

The vintage camper trailer hobby was a perfect fit for our family. We were able to enjoy classic cars and family camping time all in the same weekend. We soon became obsessed with saving every vintage trailer that we could. We immersed ourselves in the hobby and learned all we could about the different types of trailers as we rescued and restored them.

Paul had dreamed of starting a hobby paper for vintage camper trailers for a few years. Following the unexpected deaths of two family members in 2011, we reevaluated our lives and took a close look at what we wanted to accomplish.

Grace, Paul, Caroline, and Angelo Lacitinola and their 1948 Trailercraft trailer. Photo by Clay Whiteley.

camper trailer pastime has influenced the course of our lives. We have rebuilt a dozen trailers in the past ten years. We tend to be attracted to trailers that are in good original condition and can be enjoyed with minimal restoration. Patina tells a story, and we like to preserve some in order to let the trailer retain its personality. Each trailer we rebuild is unique and has its own story to share, both from the past and the present, as our family continues to make memories while enjoying these incredible pieces of history. The 1948 Trailercraft pictured here and on the preceding pages is a Masonite-

Paul, with his dogged determination and the support of the vintage camper trailer community, sent the first copy of *Vintage Camper Trailers News* off to the printer in May 2012. The original newsprint publication continued to grow each issue, and eventually graduated to a full-color, glossy magazine in 2014. To date it is the first and only magazine dedicated to the American vintage camper trailer hobby.

Our story, like so many in this book, is a testament to how the vintage

sided trailer. The interior is in unrestored, original condition. We restored the exterior and take it camping frequently. It is the only Trailercraft we have ever seen. It is one of the favorites in our collection, as it is a true representation of what the trailers looked like before they were "vintage." We love the trailers, but we thank God for the friends who have become like family as we share our love and enjoyment of vintage camper trailers.

Acknowledgments

Sonia Young's 1956 Jewel trailer (see page 194). Photo by Jason B. Lee.

It didn't take us long to realize that there would be no way to include in this book the hundreds of fabulous people we have met in the hobby. We are privileged to have so many good friends as a result of being in this hobby. We have been fortunate to see vintage trailers lovingly restored and personalized by their owners. We continue to be inspired by others, as we are in awe of their creativity.

This book is a collection of a small bit that we have encountered. We have tried to include a variety of different types of trailers and a diversity of people that realistically portray today's vintage American trailerite.

Be careful what you wish for. Writing a book is no simple task. Without Gibbs Smith's guidance and a willingness to gamble on us, this book would still just be on our to-do list. We also have to thank Caroline's mother, Nancy Veal, who proofed all of our initial drafts. She was a good sport about it and we can afford her rates.

Introduction

As we wrapped up writing this book, we reflected on the journey we have taken. We realized the trailers are the reason so many people are drawn to the hobby. They are memories of childhood for some and an artistic outlet for others. However, as we interviewed hundreds of trailerites, they've shared that the relationships they have built inside this hobby have changed their lives and kept them involved.

The diversity of those who enjoy the vintage camper trailer hobby is amazing. Doctors and dentists, homemakers and professional snowboarders, contractors and computer scientists, empty nesters, widows, widowers, singles, families, and salesmen—all have found a place to belong. With an attitude of inclusion, the hobby lacks the competitiveness found in so many other groups.

Our personal experience has been the same as those we have interviewed. This hobby gave us "family" we did not have in the area we live. Vintage camper trailer "grandparents" who've come and watched our kids—Angelo, twelve, and Grace, ten—play baseball and show their 4-H animals, as well as "aunts" and "uncles" who've taught them how to sew, fix a bike tire, frost a cupcake, and drive a motorcycle. Trailerites are the first to volunteer to help in times of crisis. When we recently had a fire near our home, our phone was ringing with offers to come tow trailers out of harm's way.

The stories we like best are those that inspire. Like the woman who shared that she was spending each evening crying after her children left her an empty nester. She had never towed before, but decided it was what she wanted to do and went for it. It is our hope that this book gives someone the push they need to join us in this crazy, fun hobby of vintage camping.

Sarah and Grant Wells during their trailer-themed wedding in front of a trailer belonging to Sarah's parents, Gary and Margot Warner (see page 96). Photo by Wendy Carr.

The Characters

Memorable for their unconventional style, these trailerites are unique in their approach to trailering and their interesting other life that makes them stand out as individuals. They are committed to the personas they portray as they enjoy the hobby in their own way. They add a special type of fun at the events they attend.

FACING: **Charles and Virginia Diffey and the "Lottie-Dah," a 1966 Scottsman (see page 30).**

Greg Tykal

Greg Tykal had a mission to find and own a Holiday House. As the owner of two vintage Airstreams, a 1964 Bambi II and a mint 1965 Safari, Greg was no stranger to the vintage camper trailer world. He had been attending rallies since 2001.

In 2009, his friends Susan and Gerry Measures shared a picture of a Holiday House and Greg fell madly in love! One year later, a mutual friend of the Measures' and Greg's brought a brochure to a rally of an old Holiday House that was for sale. The Measures passed on it, being the incredible friends that they are, and gave Greg a shot at buying the trailer. Greg called the seller and bought it sight unseen. The next day he drove to Salem, Oregon, to pick it up. He decided to sell both of his Airstreams and use the money to take time off and rebuild his dream trailer.

Greg spent a year getting the trailer ready to take to rallies. It was a showstopper. He decided to tone down the pink a bit by replacing the coral exterior with Arizona beige. Greg's passion and craftsmanship shine brightly in this beautiful time capsule. Greg is always on the lookout for rare trailers and is currently restoring a 1965 Royal Traveler by Traveleze. According to Greg, it's even more rare than a Holiday House!

Lovingly restored kitchen details in Greg Tykal's Holiday House.

The Holiday House has its own curved-wall shower stall.

Matt and Kelly Boldy

For twenty years, Matt and Kelly Boldy enjoyed the world of reenactment. Dressed as a mountain man and mountain woman, they would spend their weekends in a pre-1840s world. Reenactment is a very romantic idea until one starts getting older and no longer wants to sleep on the ground. That is what happened to the Boldys. After buying their 1974 Jet trailer, they searched the Internet looking for a group to go camping with. They found a local Tin Can Tourists event and attended. They immediately felt they belonged with the people in the vintage camper trailer hobby.

Kelly's motto is, "I don't know any strangers, just friends I haven't met yet." As president of her hometown Lions Club, Kelly exemplifies this motto. Matt is slightly more reserved

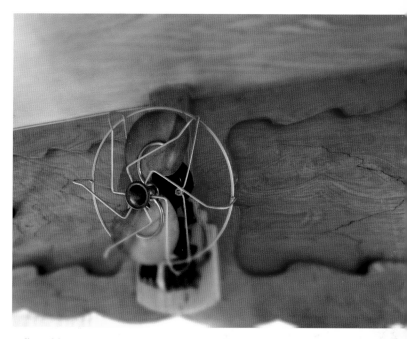

Kelly Boldy seated inside of her fan-cooled 1959 Shasta Deluxe.

and appreciates the conversation point that the vintage camper trailers have provided. After several years of camping with the Jet, they passed her on to a new family and bought a 1959 Shasta Deluxe nineteen-foot trailer and a 1947 Higgins pop-up trailer.

The Boldys, along with their daughter, Olive, are artists. Kelly makes bottle cap necklaces, key chains, and bracelets out of vintage bottle caps and sells them through her business, CAPtured Moments. Matt likes to draw pictures of hot rods and trailers, and their daughter's work can be seen in the stenciling she did in the bathroom of their Shasta. The Boldys can be seen chatting and laughing with fellow trailerites at any rally they attend.

An antique dresser topped with hammered copper and a glass bowl makes for a great washstand.

The Boldys' 1959 Shasta Deluxe has been decorated to suit Kelly's artistic taste and whimsical sense of humor.

Dal and Jane Smilie

As a young lad, Dal Smilie started camping in his backyard and continued to camp later as a Boy Scout. As he matured, he enjoyed going camping with his car or motorcycle but never really cared for trailers. Dal hated the backing up and finding a parking spot that a trailer required. For years he carried his race bikes in a truck or van so he would not have to deal with the hassle towing a trailer created.

Several years ago, while attending a large vintage motorcycle show at Del Mar, California, Dal noticed five couples with exotic vintage trailers, tow vehicles, and their early American motorcycles. Dal was shocked to see that the wives were smiling! Dal's experience with car and motorcycle shows was that the significant other was not always smiling after the first couple of hours. Dal decided there was something to learn from these couples as they sat in the shade, preparing their vintage-inspired drinks and starting up their vintage barbecue.

At vintage races in Steamboat Springs, Colorado, Dal spoke to some guys who had jammed vintage MX bikes into their Silver Streak Clipper. Later he talked to a guy who pulled his Clipper to motorcycle swap meets with a '57 Suburban. These gentlemen inspired Dal to look for his own vintage setup.

In 1997, Dal and his wife, Jane, found their 1949 Curtis Wright Clipper Model 5 outside of Palm Desert, California. The door was off and some windows were out. It was painted green, had a big swamp cooler on top, and featured 1961 plates. The Smilies struck a deal with the owners, packed the bearings, put on tires, rigged some lights, and hauled it to Montana.

Since then, Dal and his wife have towed the Curtis Wright 45,000 miles. Their main tow rig is their "resto rod," a 1948 Studebaker pickup with a towing package. Dal used to have a Studebaker pickup like this with three gallons of bulk oil stored in back to keep it going. Nothing is close in Montana, and so they have driven to California several times, Illinois, and everywhere in between. When they pull into a gas station or park at a campground, they can't get away without curious folk converging

FACING AND ABOVE: **The Smilies' 1949 Curtis Wright Clipper Model 5 being towed by their 1948 Studebaker pickup truck. Above photo submitted by Dal Smilie.**

on them and asking about their truck and trailer. Dal looks at this as an opportunity to turn folks on to vintage trailering.

The Smilies love the vintage camper trailer hobby and have hosted several rallies. Dal said, "Camping with a vintage outfit is a great way to meet great folks. Attending, volunteering, or hosting a vintage rally is an even better way!"

Bob and Jacyn Gallagher

A fellow trailerite described Jacyn and Bob Gallagher as fun-loving, accepting, generous people who just want to enjoy the sport of vintage camper trailering. What a great compliment and description of this incredible couple. Retired from the navy, Bob has time to dream, scheme, and research all things related to vintage camper trailers.

Jacyn has fond memories of camping as a child. She saw cute canned hams and continued to talk to Bob about the possibility of buying a vintage trailer and taking it camping. Bob went to work and found a 1961 Northwest Coach for sale on Craigslist. He gifted the trailer to Jacyn for her birthday in 2006. After redoing the floor and curtains they took it to their first rally: the Rollin' Oldies Vintage Trailers rally in Sweet Home, Oregon. At that first rally there were only about fifteen trailers, and one of them was owned by a friend of Bob's from high school. They had a great time reconnecting and camping.

Bob and Jacyn's hallmark is their willingness to go all out. The Gallaghers soon realized that with two teenagers camping with them, they needed a larger trailer. They found a 1957 Ideal. With its pink '50s decor, Bob wanted some clothes to match. He bought pink bowling shirts and had them embroidered with a cartoon of him, his wife, and their trailer. It was their new uniform when showing off their trailer. They also make great homemade signs describing their trailers. Bob even made a miniature version of their trailer sign for Jacyn's Christmas village.

While camping at a beach one rainy winter day, Bob and Jacyn and their friends Brian and Melissa Morrow decided to go for a drive around town to see what trailers they could see. While on their adventure they saw a two-story trailer huddled under a tarp. After knocking on doors and poking around they realized that there was someone living in it. Bob was brave enough to tour the trailer, and even though Jacyn really wanted to see the trailer as well, they both decided that it was probably a good thing that she had waited in the car, as the current occupants were rather seedy.

After Bob toured the trailer, the Gallaghers and Morrows started talking. Brian, owner of Brian's Vintage Trailers, declared

THIS PAGE AND FACING: Bob and Jacyn Gallagher's 1955 Airfloat Cruiser.

that he could build a two-story trailer. Jacyn quickly sketched out her ideas on a sheet of paper. With that, a dream was born. The Morrows and the Gallaghers collaborated, and soon Brian began building the Gallaghers the "StarKraft" using the frame of a 1950 Rollaway. Jacyn and Bob would go to swap meets on the weekends, and find bits and pieces of other vintage trailers to take to Brian to incorporate into the build. These treasures were met with many a "yeehaw" and "son of a bear!" from Brian. Nine months later, the two-story trailer was finalized, and Bob and Jacyn now have a delightful one-of-a-kind "vintage" trailer all their own.

Bob and Jacyn love to hook up one of their vintage trailers to their restored 1961 Dodge C-500 truck and hit the road. They have traveled all over the West Coast, and wherever they land they bring a special kind of Gallagher joy to the party!

Interior views of Bob and Jacyn Gallagher's "StarKraft," a completely handmade, two-story trailer, including the upstairs sleeping loft (below).

The Gallaghers' "StarKraft" is hauled by their 1961 Dodge C-500 truck.

The staircase in Bob and Jacyn Gallagher's "StarKraft."

Charles and Virginia Diffey

"Jolly," "gracious," "generous," and "kind" are words that describe Charles and Virginia Diffey. It is not far from what you would say about good old Saint Nicholas as well. Maybe because they have a close relationship.

Charles and Virginia have a zest for life. Eight years ago they started a new chapter in their adventures. Recalling fond camping memories from childhood, Virginia convinced Charles that they should buy a little vintage trailer and go camping. After looking all over California, they found their 1966 Scotsman in Fresno and towed her home. Removing the wheels and axle, Charles was able to put their new trailer on piano dollies and squeeze it into his garage with just a half-inch of clearance through the garage door. He spent a year fixing her up and making her campable. Virginia tackled the job of making the trailer adorable and naming her, and "Lottie-Dah" was given a new lease on life as a member of the Diffey family.

About the same time the vintage trailer hobby was taking off in their life, Charles was asked to be Santa at a local kindergarten class. Being the sweet guy that he is, Charles agreed. He grew his beard out for a couple of weeks, found a red and green plaid scarf, motorcycle boots, a Santa hat, and a black wool trench coat, and visited the classroom. The kids loved him and Charles found a new passion in his life. Virginia lovingly created a one-of-a-kind Victorian-era Saint Nicholas suit. Charles became a member of the Fraternal Order of Real Bearded Santas and the Central California Claus Ambassadors, for which he is currently serving as deputy chief ambassador.

Virginia Diffey's Trailer Roots

Virginia Diffey's folks were trailer people even before she was born. She shared a few snapshots and memories with us.

These are the oldest pictures of my mom and dad's car and teardrop. The back of one of the pictures is stamped that it was developed in East Liverpool, Ohio, so it was taken somewhere between California and Ohio. The other one is taken somewhere on the East Coast on the beach. At that time my brother was a toddler. They drove out from California cross-country to Vermont to visit family there for the summer, then down the East Coast, finally ending up in New Orleans for my dad's new job. They sold the teardrop and bought the next trailer in New Orleans.

This one was taken at Bayou Teche, Louisiana, when my folks were living in New Orleans. My brother remembers driving down the road in the dark next to the bayou when a tire came off the trailer and rolled into the swamp. Our dad was so mad losing his new tire that he jumped into the swamp to look for it. He was wading around in the dark in the swamp, and my brother was scared to death that a gator was going to get him. I love the way ladies dressed for camping in those days. I mean, the heels, the hat, and the dress. . . . My mother looks more like she's going to a party, not camping. After Pearl Harbor in 1941, my mother wanted to move to California so that she could be close to her mother in case the Japanese attacked the mainland, so that is why I grew up in California.

Above is a picture of my Dad and brother in another campground and again, who knows where? Can you tell that Dad is proud of his (new to him) 1940 Chevrolet Master Deluxe Sport Sedan?

This was our Corvette trailer in 1956. It was taken with my trusty little Brownie camera. Remember those?

Jimmy and Cheryl Evans

If you catch Jimmy and Cheryl Evans at a rally, it is hard not do a double take as you see their setup. Everything sparkles! Jimmy and Cheryl are do-it-yourselfers. If something needs doing, they figure out how to get it done. An accomplished custom motorcycle builder, Jimmy has an eye for making something mundane into something extraordinary.

Cheryl has always loved to ride motorcycles, starting when she was just itty-bitty. Five-year-old Cheryl convinced her grandma to cash in some savings bonds and buy her a brand new Honda 50. It's a good thing she married a bike builder! Jimmy and Cheryl own Jimmy Evans Did It in Oroville, California, where Jimmy does award-winning custom bike building. After buying a 1999 Harley-Davidson Electra Glide and a 1990 Harley-Davidson Springer, Jimmy took them straight to his shop and started cutting them up and customizing them. He said the coolest award he ever won was the Joe Bailon Elegance Award, presented annually at the San Francisco Rod, Custom and Motorcycle Show. Joe Bailon is the creator of the candy apple red paint color, and each year one vehicle wins the award based on the appearance of the paint, interior, engine, design, and suspension. A motorcycle built by Jimmy is the only bike to win this award to date.

When he was four years old, Jimmy met his best friend, Dennis Deets. Dennis had an older brother who owned a '65 El Camino. In 1983, Jimmy and Dennis were on a bike ride when Dennis was killed in an accident. At the time of the accident, Dennis and his brother were working on the El Camino. Afterwards, Dennis's brother could no longer bear to work on the El Camino and left it sitting in a barn

ABOVE: **Jimmy and Cheryl Evans and their 1957 Shasta.** BELOW: **Memorial tribute to Dennis Dean Deets, painted on the dashboard of the 1965 El Camino.**

untouched for twenty years. In 2003, Jimmy bought the car and fixed it the way his buddy would have loved to have seen it done. The El Camino now has a 496-cubic-inch, big-block four-speed and a twelve-bolt rear end. It is a piece of art.

Cheryl is Jimmy's biggest supporter and enjoys giving gifts with great meaning. In 2011, Cheryl took Jimmy on a birthday trip to pick out a new engine for the El Camino. She was also the one to find the 1957 Shasta they now tow behind the El Camino; that was a Christmas gift in 2012. After looking over the Shasta with the seller, he decided if Cheryl would just take it off his hands, he'd be happy to give it to her. So Cheryl called up her friend Carl and had him help her tow it home on rotten tires. Miraculously they made it home and Cheryl set the stage for a big Christmas surprise. With a bouquet of roses on the table and twinkling candles, Cheryl showed Jimmy his new gift. Stepping carefully to avoid the squishy spots in the floor, they enjoyed the musty odor of rotting wood as rain leaked through the ceiling. Jimmy soon had the trailer torn down and rebuilt. They towed the Shasta with the El Camino over 150 miles to attend their first rally in 2013.

Now that they had the car, the motorcycles, and the trailer, Cheryl wanted matching bicycles to complete their ensemble. Another Christmas gift was discovered when Cheryl found a vintage purple 1966 Schwinn Stingray bike. As fate would have it, a month later, in a different city, Cheryl found a matching bike with the original purple paint—a 1964 Schwinn Fiesta. It's hard to imagine what they have left to give for Christmas, but they sure do have some great stories to go along with their matching toys.

ABOVE: **Seating in the 1957 Shasta. BELOW: Restored Schwinn bikes carried in the 1965 El Camino.**

Rich Leufstedt Jr.

Rich Leufstedt Jr. is the owner of a 1961 Airstream Bambi. He is only its third owner. His parents, Richard and Diane Leufstedt, bought the trailer in 1976 after it had spent its first fifteen years being used as a New Hampshire hunting cabin. Rich's parents fixed the trailer and camped in it for another thirty-seven years. When Richard Sr. passed away in 2012, Rich Jr. inherited the trailer.

Rich Leufstedt Jr. in his 1961 Airstream Bambi. Photos (above and facing) by Ted Theodore.

When Rich brought the Bambi home to his house, he dubbed him the "Duke of Earl." Earl is a sixteen-foot Bambi, manufactured in Ohio. According to Rich, an Ohio-manufactured Bambi is more rare than those made in California. It also means that the layout is slightly different, with the bathroom on the curbside of the trailer. The Bambi sleeps two comfortably, and Rich and his wife, Cecile, enjoy taking him on weekend getaways.

An X-ray tech by day and a self-professed "ukeaholic" by night, Rich is an amazing musician. He has started using Earl as a recording studio and plans on having a new CD out shortly with songs recorded in the trailer.

Rich's stage name is "Amazing Dick" and his percussionist is "Magnificent Al." Amazing Dick can be found performing his monthly ukulele show as well as busking at local concerts. Rich also enjoys camping. He even found a girlfriend for Earl. Her name is "Loretta" and she is a 1968 Airstream Globetrotter. Unfortunately for Earl and Loretta, they have a long-distance relationship and can only see each other when their owners are camping together.

Rich loves the vintage camper trailer hobby; he can be cool *and* do things that remind him of his father: being with young people playing cribbage and pinochle at rallies, as well as sitting around jamming with them on their ukuleles and guitars.

Rich is often asked about polishing Earl. He doesn't plan on polishing him anytime soon. He loves the patina, as it shows the life his trailer has lived. If you are at a rally in New England and hear a ukulele being played, look for Amazing Dick and his trailer, Earl.

Robert Witherall and his handmade teardrop inspired by a 1946 CabinCar trailer.

Robert Witherall

Robert Witherall grew up helping his dad work on the family car. That was just the beginning of a fascination for mechanics and the automobile. For Robert, it started with a Schwinn Stingray bicycle and evolved into minibikes, motorcycles, and anything that went *fast*!

At age twenty-one, Robert fueled his fascination for cars by working at a wrecking yard. A year later, Robert's life was changed as he drove home from work. Riding his motorcycle around corners at triple the speed limit, Robert lost control and collided with a guardrail going seventy-five miles per hour. Robert recalls lying in a hospital bed, semiconscious, hearing the doctor say, "I'm sorry, son. I don't think you are going to walk again." He had broken his back and severed his spinal cord.

Robert's body was now confined to a wheelchair, but his mind was in overdrive. He was soon building racing wheelchairs and competing in 10k races and marathons. He designed and built one of the first hand-powered bicycles to compete in biathlons with able-bodied competitors.

His passion for speed fueled Robert's creativity. He enjoyed snow skiing, water skiing, jet skiing, and riding off-road vehicles. Robert built a Harley-Davidson Trike, and after attending a Goodguys car show he bought and restored a 1941 Chevrolet Master Deluxe. Captured by the '40s era, Robert replicated a 1946 wooden teardrop trailer to pull behind his hot rod. He enjoys using his teardrop at car shows as well as taking it camping.

The back end of Robert Witherall's handmade trailer.

Never one to let life pass him by, Robert continues to enjoy his many restoration projects. He is currently working on a 1949 International. He loves to restore treasures from the past and bring them back to life. He says that building motors and doing sheet-metal fabrication, body work, machining, electrical, and upholstery are all just parts of his main objective: to hear the motor roar!

Robert is no different than anyone else: he has a dream, a vision, and passion. This love of hot rods has created unique friendships and bonds with people who have made his story possible. Robert hopes to inspire others, physically limited or not. He reminds us, "Your mind is your only limitation."

Lanabelle and Ian Bogan

Lanabelle and Ian Bogan are the proud owners of an uber-custom 1964 Airstream. They spent four years and an undisclosed amount of money to make this trailer fit their own eclectic style. Influenced by the steampunk look, they incorporated ornate wooden decorations with modern fantasy-style technology.

The Airstream sports many custom upgrades that make it truly unique. Lana covered the ceiling in a tufted taupe design with silver studding. The couple went green with their 95-watt solar power setup that supports their plethora of modern technology. They incorporated a chain-link room divider, as well as vintage buttons and drawer pulls. Each of these designs lends itself to the fantasy element the couple was looking to incorporate in their restoration. Lana said she can envision her Airstream flying through the sky.

LEFT: Models Airica Michelle and Chris Yepez having fun in the Bogans' Volkswagen Golf towing their custom Airstream. ABOVE, TOP: Airica explores the cupboards in the Bogans' Airstream. ABOVE, BOTTOM: Chris chills in front of the Bogans' Airstream with an issue of Vintage Camper Trailers magazine.

The Bogans' 1964 Airstream on a sparkling
evening overlooking San Diego Bay.

Lanabelle and Ian Bogan have equipped their 1964 Airstream with everything they need to accommodate their lifestyle: interesting lighting, fabrics, finishes, and storage. Photos on pages 42-44 by Mike Lambert/Mike Madriaga. Models are Airica Michelle and Chris Yepez. Makeup and hair by Rachel Gallenberger.

Glen and Deborah Nichols

Glen and Deborah Nichols, a machinist and homemaker, respectively, are lifelong campers. As outdoor enthusiasts, they have always dreamed of owning their own cabin. While tent camping with their family, Deborah started noticing cute little vintage trailers. After attending a vintage trailer rally, Deborah started looking for her own trailer. Her son, Corey Nichols, found the 1966 Aloha for sale on Craigslist. Deborah and Corey bought the trailer and had it sitting in the yard for Glen when he returned home after

work. When Deborah informed Glen that this was their new project, he didn't have much to say and went right to work.

Glen and Deborah both agreed that they wanted to use natural materials and do the work themselves. Their trailer, "Annie Oakley," was a bit of a mess when they rescued her. She had served as a hunting shack for a man and his dog. With a ceiling that looked like a hammock, soft spots in the floor, dry rot, and a severe case of peeling paint, the Aloha was a diamond in the rough.

Tackling one issue at a time, they were soon ready for decorating their trailer. Glen had worked as a docent at Sutter's Fort in Sacramento, California, and is very knowledgeable about black powder guns and the mountain man era of the 1840s, so it was an easy decision to decorate in that style. The Nicholses refaced all the walls with knotty pinewood, covered the cabinets and cushions with real leather, and installed a new wood floor. When they pulled the contact paper off the fridge, it looked like it had been on the receiving end of target practice. Glen hammered a piece of copper and attached it to the front of the fridge. They also put copper around the sink and added some antique light fixtures. Deborah added a little lace, and Glen brought out the stripper and polish and made the exterior shine.

Now they enjoy the new friends they have made and attend several rallies a year in Annie Oakley. Their awning accentuates their mountain man decor, as they stretch a simple canvas between rough-sawn log poles. Glen and Deborah are often dressed in period-correct attire and enjoy sharing their trailer and mountain man history with anyone who stops by to admire their handiwork.

Zach and Tina Haller

Zach and Tina Haller are a young entrepreneurial couple. We met up with them at a rally where they and their daughter, Addie, had their Boles Aero trailer set up for vending some of Tina's wares. Tina is an artist and loves to create. Her shop, My Favorite Things in Nevada City, California, is full of glittery gifts and treasures. Each card, necklace, pillow, printed towel, and key chain she crafts is full of cuteness.

"I love all things old!" said Tina, when asked what inspired her to buy a vintage camper trailer. Tina loves looking for treasures at yard sales and antique shops. Her Sunday driver is a 1962 Chevrolet Impala, and Zach and Tina live in an 1872 Victorian home.

Vintage is in her blood. When Tina started to see vintage camper trailers at artist trade shows and in magazines, she started searching for her own. Tina did her research and decided that she liked the Boles Aero. Tina was very fortunate to find her Boles Aero in great shape. The outside was untouched and the previous owner

Zach and Tina Haller have filled their 1954 Boles Aero full of delightful knickknacks. Photos (facing and above) submitted by Zach and Tina Haller.

polished it for her. After making some repairs to make sure the trailer was safe, Tina started camping in her Boles.

Tina is a mom, a wife, a storeowner, a vintage camper trailerite, and a famous athlete. For twenty years (1985–2005), she was a professional snowboarder. She was constantly on the road in search of good snow and competitions. A pioneer in woman's snowboarding, Tina has won numerous awards, including a gold medal at the X Games.

The Haller family is enjoying their new hobby of vintage camper trailering, and Tina said she loves the '50s music and dancing at the rallies. Their favorite part is the escape the trailer provides. Tina shared, "It is like having board games, barbecue, and a slumber party all rolled into one!"

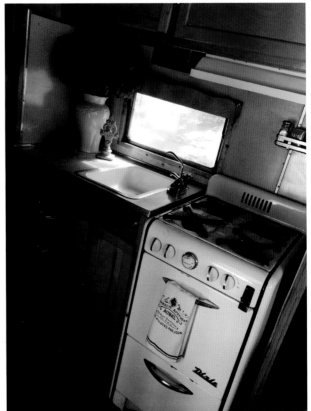

Zach and Tina Haller's Boles Aero has an expansive kitchen and dining area.

Carl and Jaime Holm

Carl and Jaime Holm fell in love with old trailers quickly, and they fell hard! Their love of trailers stemmed from both of them being born and raised on the Central Coast of California. They grew up camping and spending their childhoods constantly outdoors

"There is a lot of history on the Central Coast, long family lines, and everyone has old junk around here, as well as a lot of wide-open space," says Jaime. "We both grew up with an appreciation for the outdoors and a love of history and old things. Once we found our first trailer, there was no going back. It's like trailers have always been a part of us, whether we knew it or not."

Carl had a few old cars in high school and college, has always been real savvy with tools, and enjoys fixing things. When Carl and Jaime first met, she was living in a trailer, a single-wide to be exact. Jaime used to travel quite a bit, and lived in a trailer on two different occasions after high school. Her love of trailers and life on the road was cemented when she lived in a caravan in Australia for a while. As Jaime put it, "The simplicity of having everything you need, right there with you, was so freeing . . . I couldn't imagine living any other way."

Once Carl and Jaime got together, their combined interest of traveling, life on the road, and old things quickly spawned an idea. In 2012, Tinker Tin Trailer Co. was born. Jaime had just turned twenty-five years old, and Carl thirty-three; they had just gotten married a few months prior, and bought their first trailer with the idea to start fixing them up and renting them out for other people to enjoy the lifestyle that they loved so much. What started out as a simple idea to fix up one trailer quickly turned into a fleet of more than thirty trailers, including 1930s Hayes and Masonite homebuilt trailers, 1940s Westcrafts and Curtis Wrights, and classic 1950s Jewels, Aljoas, Kenskills, Crowns, Shastas, and Terry canned hams, to name a few. Some of the trailers in their collection are simply period pieces to honor the time, while others are fully restored

campers for rent, vintage bar and vending trailers, and vintage trailer photo booths.

"Anyone who has an old trailer knows it turns into a sickness. You fall so in love with the trailers, and their stories and their history, and you can't help but want to save them all. These trailers are a big part of our American history, and once they are gone, they are never coming back. Preserving them has become so important for us!"

Photo submitted by Carl and Jaime Holm.

Marti Domyancic

Vintage camper trailers have taken over Marti Domyancic's business. For the last thirty years, Marti primarily upholstered cars, motorcycles, airplanes, and trucks at her home-based upholstery business. After a friend dropped off a 1947 Kit teardrop at her doorstep, Marti entered the world of vintage camper trailers. Marti took the Kit apart and used it for a pattern, completely rebuilding the teardrop. While attending a rally, Marti saw a need for custom awnings. She looked at the trailers and their awnings and said, "I can make those!"

With that simple thought, Marti's Trailer Awnings opened its doors for business. Sewing her first custom awning in 2008, Marti's business blossomed. Within a year, Marti no longer was upholstering, because she had so many orders for awnings. Word has spread and Marti now has orders for awnings from all over the world. She ships everywhere, from Wisconsin and Michigan, to New Zealand, Australia, Norway, France, and Sweden. Marti laughed as she said people are shocked when she answers the phone or calls them back for order details. She is still a one-woman powerhouse running her business by herself.

Watching Marti have such a great time at rallies spurred Marti's sisters to want to camp with her. The '47 Kit was not large enough for family to join her camping, so Marti and her son Trevor took on another project in 2010. They bought and restored a 1960 Shasta. Months of hard work paid off and Marti now enjoys camping and rallying in her Shasta. She delights in having her sisters, Shirley and Cindy, her husband, Bob, and their grandchildren join her when she goes camping and to rallies. She has taken six of her eight grandkids camping, and is just waiting for the last two to be a bit older before taking them out as well.

If you ever attend a rally and see vintage-inspired awnings adorning the vintage camper trailers, chances are they have been sewn by Marti.

Marti Domyancic makes awnings, like this one for her own 1960 Shasta.

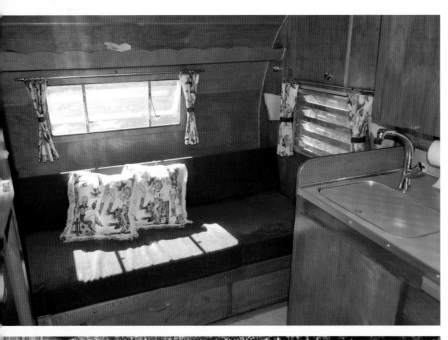

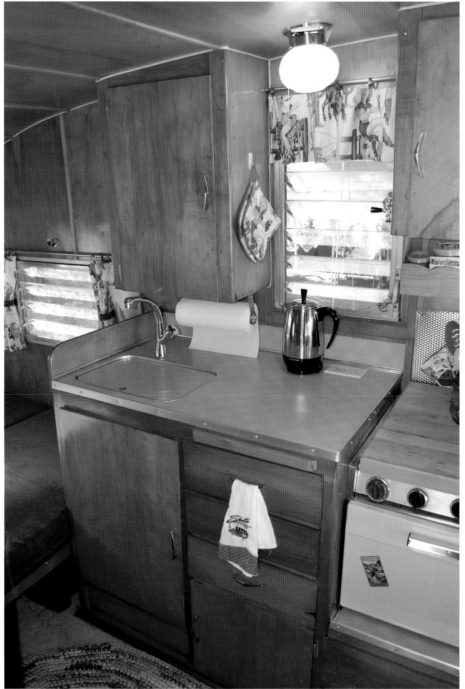

Charlie Nienow and Penny Cotter

Charlie Nienow and Penny Cotter love to go camping, hunting, fishing, and diving for abalone along the Northern California coast. Charlie is an automotive painter and Penny runs a family childcare business out of their home. Their family are hot-rodders, and Penny felt with their love of the outdoors and hot rods that a vintage camper trailer would be a perfect fit for their lifestyle.

After a bit of cajoling and pleading from Penny, Charlie decided he should help her pick out a trailer. Penny found several potential trailers before Charlie agreed on one to purchase in 2006: a 1962 Shasta Airflyte. For Penny it was love at first sight. Charlie was a little more reserved about their new acquisition.

For six months they had the Shasta parked in their front yard while they fixed it up. When the trailer first arrived, the neighbors thought they were crazy. Soon the trailer became a neighborhood project, as their neighbors would come by daily to look at their progress and talk shop.

Now they have a beautifully restored Shasta that they take to rallies and on many family adventures. Penny enjoys having a

nice place to sleep, recalling previous camping adventures sleeping in a tent and waking up in puddles of water. Charlie and Penny are very active in the vintage camper trailer world and host two rallies each year.

RIGHT: Charlie and Queen Penny in front of their 1962 Shasta Airflyte.

The Collectors

Collectors of vintage camper trailers tend to be eccentric. The ones featured here have amassed anywhere from four to nearly forty trailers in their collections. Whether they gravitate to a particular brand, a certain era, or are forever chasing after the elusive barn find, most will tell you the hunt is as satisfying as the acquisition. On the following pages, these individuals share their passion for preserving America's past for future generations to enjoy.

FACING: **A portion of the Katkowsky collection (see page 68), including their 1961 Holiday House (left), 1927 Holt Prototype, and 1951 Vagabond (right).**

John and Phyllis Green

In 1998, John and Phyllis Green sold their large "new" trailer because they didn't have room for it at their home. They then bought a 1946 Kit teardrop while attending an antique show. After attending a few rallies they were hooked, and were soon rescuing vintage camper trailers.

Their first rescue was a 1952 Silver Streak Clipper. John and Phyllis worked together at restoring this trailer to as near its original condition as possible. After several years of camping in the '52 Silver Streak Clipper, they again had storage space issues and decided to sell it. The trailer was purchased by the president of the Japanese Airstream group and shipped overseas.

Over the past eighteen years, John and Phyllis have rescued ten trailers, each of which was discovered while driving the backroads of California. The Greens have an exceptional eye for

ABOVE: **John and Phyllis Green.**
BELOW AND FACING: **The Greens' 1947 Aero Flite.**

1948 Westwood Coronado.

finding antiques to match the time period of their trailers. The ironic part of the Greens' story is that what first caused them to get into this hobby—their lack of storage space—has only been exacerbated with their solution to the original problem. Now they truly *are* out of storage space!

The Greens' current collection includes:

● **1947 Aero Flite** While doing restoration work for a friend, John needed some parts. On his way to RV Doctor George, a parts and service clinic, he noticed the Aero Flite sitting in a yard. He spoke to the owner, a junk hauler, who had realized the Aero Flite was unique and had hauled it to his house instead of to a recycler. John soon purchased the Aero Flite from him.

● **1948 Westwood Coronado** Driving around during a campout, John spotted the trailer in a woman's yard. He kept in contact with her for a year before she decided to sell.

1949 Traveleze While attending the one hundred fiftieth anniversary celebration of the discovery of Calaveras Big Trees, the Greens met the original owner of the Traveleze. When the owner told the Greens about his trailer, John offered to buy it. Not ready to sell at the time, he stayed in touch and wound up purchasing the trailer a year later.

1950 Kamp Master Tipped off by fellow trailerites Wayne and Kathy Ferguson that this trailer was for sale, the Greens went to look at what they thought was a traditional teardrop. When they arrived, they found the Kamp Master, and didn't hesitate to buy it and haul it home.

1950 Westcraft Coronado Trolley Top The Greens found the Trolley Top on their way to an almond festival. John spotted this trailer and knocked on its door. He bought the trailer from the second owner.

1957 Airstream Bubble John was picking up parts for another trailer restoration project when he saw a man trying to unlock an Airstream Bubble in the parking lot. Knowing how fragile and expensive vintage door

1950 Kamp Master teardrop.

handles can be, John offered to help. It turned out that the man was the second owner of the Bubble; he had a sentimental attachment to the trailer and wasn't ready to sell. Again, John kept in touch, and when the time was right to sell, John and Phyllis were there to buy it.

Authors' Note: As a lover of old things, Paul had bought our family a small vintage trailer to take our babies camping. We soon realized that people enjoyed seeing these older trailers on the road. Paul started writing a column about vintage camper trailers for a local car hobby paper, *Cruisin' News*. In one of his columns he suggested that other owners of vintage trailers in the Sacramento area should contact him. Phyllis Green contacted Paul and told him that a small group of vintage camper trailer owners were going to be camping together at the Stockton Delta KOA campground near Lodi, California. Paul and our daughter, Grace, went down and met Phyllis and her husband, John. It is easy to say that this encounter with the Greens changed our lives. We soon realized we had found "our people," and that we hadn't been the ones to invent vintage camper trailering. Everyone has someone who has shown them the way of the vintage camper trailer hobby. For our family, John and Phyllis Green were just that; these folks were experts!

THIS PAGE AND FACING: **John and Phyllis Green's 1950 Westcraft Coronado Trolley Top trailer.**

Mike and Zellie Perini

Mike and Zellie Perini have been rescuing and restoring vintage camper trailers since 2007. They continue to bring amazing pieces of history back to life.

A collector of extraordinary measures, Mike Perini is a super-nice, one-of-a-kind guy. His workmanship shines in his 1959 Airstream Comet. The Comet had been in his wife Zellie's family since the 1980s. Zellie gave the trailer to her daughter after buying a new trailer. The trailer was well used and loved for a couple of years, but soon, with the addition of a couple more kids, the little family outgrew it. The Comet sat unused for more than twenty-three years at their daughter's home.

When Mike was offered a chance to rebuild it, he decided to keep it as close to the original

Mike and Zellie Perini's 1959 Airstream Comet.

as he could to help keep memories alive. This little trailer needed a complete restoration from the floor up. Mike said the mice had decided to use it for a breeding ground; he found twenty-seven mice nests while cleaning it out.

Each trailer has a special story, and this one is extraordinary. Mike and Zellie have very special memories of their two grandchildren. Mike recalled how their daughter and son-in-law used two pieces of plywood over the trailer's bathtub to make a little bed for their grandchildren to sleep on. When their thirteen-year-old granddaughter passed away tragically, she left a gaping hole in all of their lives. Just before starting the restoration on the trailer, their nine-year-old grandson also passed away. However, Mike told me he and his wife try to remember the joy that their grandchildren brought to their lives every day; there is not a day that goes by that they are

Mike and Zellie Perini | 65

not remembered. The wood that was lovingly used to make the children's bed was incorporated into the restoration of the trailer. Mike and Zellie both agree that this trailer will never be sold. "It is a piece of our family," said Zellie. When Mike and Zellie pass on, the trailer will be given back to their daughter, and her kids and grandkids.

RIGHT: **Mike and his 1959 Mobylette made by Motobécane in France.**

Mike Perini's 1948 Oldsmobile with a 1947 Kenskill teardrop.
Photo submitted by Mike and Zellie Perini.

Steve and Jenay Katkowsky

Extraordinary collectors of antiques and vintage nostalgia, Steve and Jenay Katkowsky have their own museum. When you enter their home and museum it is difficult to know what to look at first: old swimsuits, head vases (ceramic vases used by florists in the '40s and '50s that featured the head or bust of a person), vintage luggage, or camping gear. Each item is amazing, and most are accompanied with a story of how and where the treasure was acquired.

Steve has always had an eye for fantastic collectibles. He has been collecting cars and memorabilia for more than forty years. His first trailer was purchased from a man in Florida. After finding an ad in *Hemmings Motor News* for a 1953 Vagabond that had never been lived in, Steve contacted the seller. Leery that it was not as perfect as the

Steve and Jenay Katkowsky's garage is jam-packed with vintage cars, camping gear, and trailers, including the rare 1961 Trailorboat (left).

seller had described, he decided to fly to Florida to take a look at the thirty-five-foot trailer. He said that when he finally saw the trailer, it was amazing. It really had never been lived in, and was in mint condition.

Steve is a funny guy. As a lecturer, both nationally and internationally, he has some great one-liners. He makes jokes constantly about his and his wife's hoarding, and anything else that he finds entertaining. Basically, he has a joke for everything. Steve and Jenay share true love and bring balance to each other's lives. Married for forty-seven years, they have traveled the world together and enjoyed collecting great vintage pieces. During a rare moment of seriousness, Steve shook his head and said he really would be nothing without Jenay. Now, when he lectures men on how to get their wives excited about old cars, he encourages them to buy a vintage trailer.

Steve and Jenay's collection includes:

● **1951 Vagabond Model 232** This trailer was found by the same man who sold Steve and Jenay their original thirty-five-foot Vagabond. After selling their original vintage camper trailer, they went on a search for a smaller trailer that had a bathroom. Steve found it. Though Model 232 Vagabonds did not come with bathrooms, back in 1951 the original owner

Steve and Jenay Katkowsky have restored this 1961 Holiday House.

called the manufacturer and had them add a bathroom while it was being built in the factory. This is currently the only known Model 232 Vagabond with a bathroom. It is the main trailer Steve and Jenay use when camping—their personal favorite.

● **1961 Holiday House** Full of rot, this trailer was renovated with artistic flair. It confirms Steve's incredible restoration skills and shows off the futuristic style of the '60s.

● **1940 Vagabond Model 16** This is a Masonite trailer still in original condition. The original owner purchased the trailer to live in for three months while his home was being built. After his home was finished, he put the trailer under cover and let it sit. When he passed away, the new owners of the property wanted to get rid of the trailer. Steve happened to be the lucky buyer. He has never touched the outside. He wants to leave it in the same condition he found it, just to prove that those elusive barn finds we all dream about can still be discovered!

● **1961 Trailorboat** This was another trailer that required Steve's restoration expertise. Full of holes and jagged cutout fenders, massive fiberglass repair was required. Once the trailer was restored, Steve and Jenay painted it to match their 1954 Cadillac convertible.

● **1927 Holt Prototype** Jenay gets the kudos for rescuing this one-of-a-kind trailer. While on vacation, she told Steve that she had seen a trailer under a tarp. After waiting several days to meet the owners, they were told the trailer had just been pulled from a barn one week before it was spotted by Jenay. At that time, the trailer was not for sale. Steve's monthly phone calls and persistence paid off a year later when the family finally agreed to let him take it home and restore

Steve and Jenay Katkowsky's wonderfully warm 1940 Vagabond Model 16.

it. Steve has restored the Holt only to the same point that Mr. Holt had built it to. The bottom of a drawer is still missing, as it was when it was purchased. The Holt Prototype is the oldest known unused trailer. Steve has no plans for this trailer to ever leave his museum.

● **1946 Slumbercoach** This trailer was manufactured by Wesley in Glendale, California. It was in storage for years. It's a completely original "woody" teardrop, down to the light fixtures and the stove. Steve and Jenay tow it with their '49 Plymouth woody wagon. There are less than a half dozen of these trailers.

Steve and Jenay Katkowsky have carefully restored this amazing, one-of-a-kind trailer—a 1927 Holt Prototype.

Steve and Jenay Katkowsky also own this handsome 1946 Slumbercoach teardrop.

Steve and Jenay Katkowsky like to use their 1954 Cadillac convertible to tow their 1951 Vagabond Model 232.

Vince Martinico

Vince Martinico has been a "horse trader" forever. He started collecting stamps and wheat pennies when he was five years old. He has bought, sold, traded, and collected his entire life. Nineteen and newly married, Vince and his wife, Karen, were living in a Chevy pickup truck with a camper shell in Montana. It was November and they were facing a cold winter. Vince started knocking on doors to see if he could find a cabin to buy or rent for the season. He found a sweet lady willing to rent her summer home: a thirty-three-foot 1950s trailer. This was Vince's first encounter with vintage camper trailers.

Ten years later, he saw an old Bowlus at a swap meet. He spoke with the owner, who told him that these trailers were so rare Vince would never find another one. That was all it took for Vince! The hunt was on. At twenty-nine, he began collecting these one-of-a-kind vehicles. Vince is known for his incredible collection. His goal is to open a museum and share his trailer treasures with the public. He is still searching for a building that will house the museum.

Vince is a private collector and graciously allowed us to share this single photo of one of his storage barns. He is a walking encyclopedia on prewar trailers and house cars from the 1930s and early 1940s. He knows the backstory on every single trailer he owns. He restores his trailers to as original condition as possible. Vince said that over the last thirty years, "I couldn't start to estimate how many trailers I have found and pulled out of barns, fields, lean-tos, garages, etc., all for the love and history of these great old trailers." Now Vince has passed the passion for picking on to his son, Dominic, and they continue to find incredible trailers together.

Justin and Anna Scribner

Justin and Anna Scribner have always been drawn to midcentury Americana. As admirers of vintage cars, clothing, and motorcycles, as well as owners of a midcentury home, the Scribners had their eyes open for vintage treasures. In the late '90s, when Justin found an ad for a 1958 Shasta Airflyte, Anna reluctantly agreed to go take a look at the vintage trailer. She shared that she was thinking mold and peeling paneling when she heard about it. Thankfully, Justin could visualize the finished product, and being a contractor was able to restore the Airflyte. The Scribners spent five years camping in their Shasta and making wonderful memories. As dog owners, they loved being able to take their own space with them when they traveled.

As the recession hit the United States, being a contractor made it difficult to pay the bills, as building nearly stopped. Having fallen in love with vintage camper trailers—their design and craftsmanship—Justin and Anna decided to open their own restoration shop. In 2010, Flyte Camp, named after their original trailer, opened its doors for service. In just five years they have restored dozens of trailers, as well as becoming reality TV personalities featured on the Great American Country network series *Flippin' RVs*.

Justin and Anna are grateful for the opportunity to preserve and restore American history. When they first started in the hobby, they were able to find "time-capsule" trailers that were left untouched for forty, fifty, or even sixty years. After the Scribners rescued these trailers, they would open the doors and cupboards to see clothes still hanging in the closets, soap and razors in the medicine cabinets, and newspapers from the last outing. It was easy for them to imagine what their parents and grandparents had experienced. It was authentic and it kept the Scribners wanting to see more. Now, as the hobby has grown, there are fewer trailers sitting in fields waiting to be discovered. Justin and Anna are grateful to be part of the vintage camper trailer movement that is helping to preserve this part of America's past for future generations to enjoy. And they and their son, Sullivan, continue to enjoy camping in their vintage trailers.

Justin and Anna Scribner with their 1947 Buick 50 convertible and 1950 Crown travel trailer. Photo submitted by Justin and Anna Scribner.

Will and Kellie Ward

Will and Kellie Ward, along with their son, William, are avid vintage camper trailerites. Will is an artist who has designed and built many art pieces as well as his custom home. He first started restoring vintage camper trailers in 2002, when the family decided they needed to go camping. They knew they did not want to own a "white box," and went on the hunt for a midcentury modern trailer that more fit their style. They found a 1962 Silver Streak that they put a Christopher Deam interior into, having salvaged it from a totaled Airstream. Will and Kellie took the trailer to their first rally, where they were asked if the trailer was for sale. Even though they said it wasn't, they ended up selling it by the end of the weekend. The Wards realized that there could be something to restoring trailers, and started their own restoration business.

As an artist, Will does what works for him when he restores a trailer. He enjoys doing his own design, and therefore only does spec trailers so he can have the freedom to create the finished product that he has envisioned. Will says he is "basically doing this for himself." After he builds a trailer, there always seems to be someone who can't live without it, and then Will is on to another creation.

Kellie, a registered nurse, helps Will with a "little bit of everything." After her sixty-hour work week she enjoys doing whatever it takes to complete their latest project. William is always hanging around with his dad helping restore the trailers, making it a real family hobby. The family focuses on midcentury Spartan trailers. They enjoy the camping and the restoring.

Will, Kellie, and son William with their recently restored 1951 Glider.

THIS PAGE AND FACING:
Most of the warm wood in this trailer was in decent condition, even though the trailer was found abandoned in a field and a home to pigeons for many years. Will built the polished bathroom and had to replace the entire rotted living room floor.

The Families

Many of the more seasoned trailerites reminisce about what they remember about camping and the campers they had growing up. Now we have the opportunity to create memories like that for the next generation. The families featured in this section are doing just that: sharing the joy of rescuing, restoring, and rallying with their kids and grandkids.

FACING **The Rogers (left to right): Adelyn, Michelle, Kyle, Alec, and Amriel (see page 101). Photo submitted by Michelle and Kyle Rogers.**

Jerry and Charlene Cecil / Dave and Connie Miller / Rick Elliott

Jerry and Charlene Cecil and the trailer that started it all, a Boles Aero.

In 2009, Jerry and Charlene Cecil bought a little trailer for Jerry to take out to the Bonneville Salt Flats to have a place to stay at the races. It needed a lot of work, and Charlene roped her son, Rick Elliott, into helping her restore it. Soon, the amount of work that Charlene had invested in the tiny Boles Aero trailer made it "their" trailer instead of just "his."

Work friends of Jerry's and Charlene's saw the fun they were having in their trailer and found their own. In 2010, Dave and Connie Miller found their 1947 Boles Aero abandoned in a boneyard in Hornbrook, California. Years of restoration and hours of hard work paid off for both couples, as they had the pleasure of taking a Route 66 trip across the United States in 2012.

By this time, the Cecils understood what a treasure they had found in their Boles Aero. So in 2013, when Rick found a 1947 Boles Aero on Craigslist, he scooped it up and got to work completely restoring it. After gutting and rewiring it, installing new insulation, and redoing the woodwork, Rick joined the Boles Aero group and is enjoying camping and rallying.

ABOVE AND BELOW: **Next came Dave and Connie Miller's sixteen-foot 1947 Boles Aero.**

ABOVE AND BELOW: **Finally, Rick Elliott and his 1947 Boles Aero.**

Bruce and Heather Phillips

Bruce and Heather Phillips and their children, Nate and Eliza, were enjoying their first rally in 2015 when we met them. In 2003, with a new baby on the way, they decided that a trailer would be a good way to continue camping without setting up and hauling the six tons of required baby gear into a tent. They found their 1954 Aljoa Sportsman and sent it to a restorer for a light renovation. Unfortunately, it took eight years for them to get their trailer back!

When they purchased the trailer, Bruce and Heather were thinking that its fourteen-foot size would work perfectly for their little family. The trailer did work well on its maiden camping trip to Yellowstone in 2013, but it was a bit tight with two tweens on board. They had a great time stopping at state parks and crazy roadside attractions during their three-week journey.

ABOVE AND BELOW: **The interior of the Phillips' 1954 Aljoa Sportsman.**
RIGHT: **Bruce, Eliza, and Heather Phillips (left to right).**

Lacey and Josh Holder

ABOVE: **The Holders and their 1970 trailer.** BELOW: **A tabletop map helps the family plan their next move. Photos (above and below) by Ramsey Harrison.**

Lacey and Josh Holder, a homemaker and electrical technician from northwest Missouri, wanted to take their children camping and found themselves drawn to vintage camper trailers. They started taking pictures and researching the possibilities of buying a restored trailer, but discovered the price of a restored vintage camper trailer was outside of their budget. So they decided to look for a trailer they could restore themselves. They found and purchased a 1970 camper trailer.

As they started replacing the floor they soon realized their trailer needed a lot more than a light restoration. Though it was not in their original plan, this young family did a complete restoration on their trailer. Following the restoration, Lacey and Josh and their children, Keegan and Riahlynn, took their maiden camping voyage. The family had an amazing time floating down a river and camping. They plan on making many more memories in their vintage camper trailer.

Jason and Rachael Ellison

Jason Ellison loves the outdoors and wanted to start camping more, but his wife, Rachael, wasn't quite as enthusiastic about the idea—specifically the woods, bugs, or hiking. She was pregnant with their son, Oliver, and was often chasing around their little girl, Gwendolyn. Jason soon realized that the only way he was going to get his wife to go camping was to buy a trailer.

Jason has always liked older things, so being the frugal fellow that he is, he decided that he would find an older trailer to fix up and use rather than buy one of those "behemoth white giants" you see going down the road. The vintage style fit into the Ellisons' approach to life: Jason tries to go with the "oldies but goodies" whenever he can. From the straight razor he uses in the morning to the reel mower he pushes in the afternoon sun, Jason loves vintage. It reminds him of a time when America had pride in itself.

Jason searched on the Internet, looked in backyards, woodlots, and empty fields. One day his mother-in-law called him to say she had found a 1965 BeeLine Wasp sitting on the side of the road with a For Sale sign. It was only $500! When Jason went to look at the

ABOVE: **The 1965 BeeLine Wasp as found by Jason.** BELOW: **Oliver and Gwendolyn Ellison.**

trailer, he found it had been sitting for some time and was infested with mice and vines. It was super stinky, and Jason needed his mother-in-law's encouragement and optimism to offer the owner even $250 for the Wasp. The owner agreed with the price, and Jason towed the trailer home—very slowly.

The BeeLine Wasp sat for the first winter while Jason dreamed about what he needed to accomplish to get the trailer ready for camping. The frigid Vermont winter didn't provide much motivation to restore the trailer, with two to three feet of snow on the ground. However, he got busy online and ordered most of the necessary parts. While looking for parts, he found *Vintage Camper Trailers News* and subscribed in time to receive the very first issue. Jason said, "That is when I figured out this vintage trailer thing is a little bigger than I thought. Imagine that! I am not the only weirdo after all!"

As soon as it got warm enough, Jason was busting his hump to get the trailer restored in time for their upcoming church camp. Every spare moment was spent working on the trailer. Jason's in-laws gifted them a

The Ellisons restored their 1965 BeeLine Wasp, outfitting the tiny space with all of the comforts of home.

Now the Ellisons camp out in this 1975 Apache Ramada trailer. With sleeping wings extended, it is twenty feet long.

professional paint job for their "new" trailer. Gwendolyn enjoyed supervising the project from her playpen and "helping" her dad fix the trailer. Three months of hard work and $3,500 later, the BeeLine Wasp was finished. Jason met his goal, and the BeeLine was ready just in time for church camp.

For a while Jason towed his vintage trailer with a 1966 Ford pickup, but with two growing kids the Ellisons needed to sell their tow rig and their trailer in order to find space for all four of them. Their current trailer is a 1975 Apache Ramada. It is a twenty-foot camper with room for this young family to grow.

Now the Ellisons go camping a couple of times a month and attend vintage camper trailer rallies whenever they have the opportunity. They love camping as a family. They've met a lot of great friends through the vintage camper trailer hobby. They continue to camp out with those friends, and enjoy meeting up at car shows and other events as well. Jason joined the Tow Boyz Vintage Camper Trailers Club, and became president of the Green Mountain (Vermont) chapter.

The Apache Ramada has all the room Oliver and Gwendolyn require.
All photos pages 90-93 by Laurie Walters of Walters Photography.

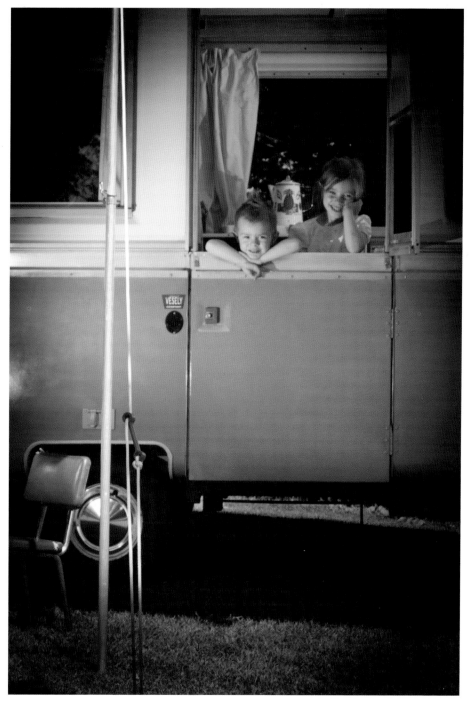

Kassandra Munro

In 2010, Kassandra Munro was with her great-grandmother, Nanny, when her grandparents, Charlie and Delores Munro (Grammy and Papa), brought home their first trailer, a 1950 Crown. Nanny said to her, "Kassy, let me tell you my story about traveling in an old travel trailer." What follows is the story of her family and their love for old trailers—but most of all it's about Kassy's great-grandmother, Nanny, her love for her family, and how five generations of Munros got involved in "those old trailers."

In 1939 and 1940, Nanny, her sister, and her father (Kassy's great-great-grandfather) traveled to revivals throughout the Midwest. Kassy's great-great-grandfather was a Pentecostal minister. Some days they would stop at the cotton fields, and Nanny would cook and sell lunches to the cotton pickers. Sometimes in their trailer she would cook for as many as thirty workers, selling them a hot lunch for twenty-five cents. Nanny and her sister slept in the back bed and their dad slept on the table area. They pulled that trailer with a Model A pickup truck. Nanny couldn't remember what kind of a trailer it was, but later, when Kassy was eleven years old and got her own 1952 Boles Aero, Nanny told her that their trailer had looked like that.

In 2003, Kassy's Aunt Shari and Uncle Pete (Shari and Pete Perry) got a 1964 Scotsman. And in 2010, Kassy's Aunt Liz and Uncle Barry (Liz and Barry Marks) bought a Cardinal. The Cardinal had been sitting just a half

Nanny and Kassandra Munro.

Kassandra Munro has surrounded her Boles Aero with gladiolas and irises. Photos (facing and above) submitted by Kassandra Munro.

mile from Grammy's house, and Kassy found it while riding her quad.

In 2011, Grammy and Papa's neighbor gave them a 1948 Kenskill (the Kenskill is now in a private car museum in Colorado). In May 2011, they took the Kenskill to a Pismo Beach rally. Papa bought a motor home so it was easier for eighty-nine-year-old Nanny to go with them. Nanny loved that she could use the bathroom while the motor home was going sixty miles an hour down the road. Aunt Liz, Uncle Barry, Uncle Pete, Kassy's cousin Bradley, Papa, Grammy, and Nanny all went to the rally, making four generations of Munros in attendance.

In 2012, Kassy got her Boles Aero, and the family went to the Pismo Beach rally again. And again they had four generations at the rally, including Nanny. While they were at Pismo Beach, a friend of Aunt Liz's wanted to buy Kassy's trailer. She told him no; she didn't want to sell it. Then he said to her, "Will you marry me?" Kassy knew he just wanted her trailer. All the trailers that the family first acquired came from somewhere in Nevada.

Kassy's dad is a car guy, so he got a 1966 Low Liner, because it goes with his truck. But Kassy thinks her Boles is way cooler. She shares her Boles with Papa and Grammy, and tries to go to as many rallies as she can. Sometimes, Nanny, Grammy, and she would go to estate sales to find things for the trailers. When they would buy something, Nanny would say, "I used to have one of those," and they would all laugh.

In 2013, Nanny had an operation. Kassy used to have lunch and sometimes dinner with her when she was in the hospital. They would talk about the trailer, and how her whole family loved these old trailers. She would tell everyone at the hospital that Kassy had a trailer just like the one her father and she had way back in 1939.

The family lost Nanny in 2014, but Kassy knows she is up in heaven, watching her and thinking, "Kassy, let me tell you my story. In 1939, my family had one of 'those old trailers . . .'"

Gary and Margo Warner / Sarah and Grant Wells

It was a perfect storm for Gary and Margo Warner. In 2005, Margo joined Sisters on the Fly and wanted her own trailer. Through *RV Trader*, they located a 1970 Red Dale in Red Bluff, California. Gary started researching and soon found that he, too, could get excited about these little trailers. An electrician and craftsman by trade, Gary saw potential in the forgotten trailers he found once he started looking. Walking through his barn he pointed out the six chosen trailers that he and Margo plan on keeping out of the dozens they have rescued. When asked where he gets all his trailers, Gary humbly shrugs and says, "They just show up!" He feels it is his job to match these lost trailers with people who will rescue them and bring them back to life.

Gary and Margo work hard to rescue these treasures, doing whatever it takes to get them. Gary spent a week wiring a bed and breakfast in exchange for their nineteen-foot 1950s Vagabond and a 1941 Westcraft. Rather than go into town every night, Gary opted to sleep in his car while working at the remote job site—and almost gave his life when he forgot that bears love toothpaste. After a long day of work, Gary brushed his teeth and took his contacts out, and was just going to sleep when he heard snorting. Rubbing his eyes, he glanced up to see a bear's nose pressed against the driver's side window. The bear searched

for a way to get into the car for several minutes while Gary sat frozen in the front seat. After the bear startled and moved off, Gary decided to make that drive into town and sleep next to the fire station.

Gary and Margo's daughter, Sarah, was married to Grant Wells in August 2014. The family property has a beautiful view of Tehachapi, California. Sarah and Grant decided it would make a great location for their wedding and reception. With Gary's incredible ability at rescuing trailers, there were plenty of vintage camper trailers to decorate the location. At that time, Sarah and Grant were restoring their own 1963 Oasis camper trailer to join Gary and Margo in the hobby. While planning a wedding and restoring their '63 Oasis, Sarah and Grant casually commented that they would like a trolley top trailer. Gary and Margo took this little nugget of information and made their dream a reality when they found and gave their kids this special trailer as a wedding gift.

With most collectors, the hunt is never really over. Gary still enjoys driving backroads and looking over fences to see if he can find that one perfect trailer or help locate a lost trailer that still needs to be rescued.

ABOVE: **Sarah and Grant Wells pose with their wedding gift from Grant and Margot Warner, a fixer-upper trolley top.**
BELOW: **Some of the Warners' future projects. All photos on pages 96-97 by Wendy Carr.**

Rita and Steve Babcock

Generational camping! Rita and Steve Babcock and their son, Chris, are a delightful family. What makes them unique is that Chris is twenty-nine and has joined his parents in their love of vintage camping.

In 2008, Rita and Steve attended a Prosser Farm Chicks barn dance, where there were several trailers set up for folks to enjoy. Steve had been trying to convince Rita that they needed to get a vintage trailer to restore. Rita said as soon as she saw those cute trailers she no longer felt her husband was crazy, and was ready to have a trailer of their own. Their first restoration was a 1964 Aloha.

This little fourteen-foot trailer needed a lot of love. They learned how to do most of the work on their own, and even found a second Aloha to use for spare parts. They did everything except the upholstery and paint. Chris helped his dad with the interior wood restoration, and learned along with his mom how to polish aluminum . . . which teaches patience!

"We learned a lot doing our first trailer; it's not perfect but we love it!" said Rita.

The Babcocks' first project, a 1964 Aloha.

The Babcocks took about a year and a half to get her ready to camp. Now they are enjoying camping and are having their 1956 Yellowstone restored by their friend Ben Santjer.

When Steve found a 1955 Westates San Gabriel in a field in Quincy, Washington, he knew it would be the perfect first restoration project for Chris. The owner of the trailer lived in Seattle, and Steve kept calling the owner until he finally agreed to sell (as soon as duck season was over). Chris spent almost a year stripping off the house paint, taking all the windows out, resealing and polishing them, polishing the exterior, and re-creating the San Gabriel decal from ghost images he saw etched in the paint.

The Babcocks are one talented family who are definitely infected with the vintage trailer bug. Chris is now working on his second trailer, a 1959 Shasta Deluxe. He found this trailer, which had originally belonged to the owners' grandparents, and spent a few weeks convincing them to sell it. After learning that Rita had gone to school with one of the grandkids who owned it, they finally agreed to sell. The

Interior of the Babcocks' 1964 Aloha.

trailer was very dirty (one window was broken, and birds and mice were living in it), but the wood inside was nearly perfect, since it had been under cover. It even still had the original shower curtain in it! Chris has been busy sanding the interior of the Shasta and replacing the curled-up floor tiles.

The entire Babcock family continues to enjoy the hobby, as they rebuild trailers and plan on hosting their first rally.

The Babcocks' second project was this 1955 Westates San Gabriel.

Michelle and Kyle Rogers

For the Rogers' very first trip in their Avion, they took a four-day camping excursion to Campland on the Bay in San Diego. They had so much fun, and finally felt like they were a part of the camping world! The Rogers were a little apprehensive about a couple of things initially, as they had never towed nor camped before, and were also curious to see whether *all five members* of the family (see page 84) would be able to sleep comfortably.

They took full advantage of the cot/hammock wood inserts that were originally in the trailer and sewed a "bed" for their middle daughter out of canvas. Thankfully, they were all able to sleep just fine! The shower, toilet, and original vintage stove all worked great, too. They purchased the awning from Marti's Trailer Awnings.

They were probably the *only* vintage trailer among a sea of gigantic RVs, and they sure got a lot of attention and stares. People loved the Rogers' trailer and even asked to see the inside. They are now happy to be new members of the vintage camper family.

All photos this page submitted by Michelle and Kyle Rogers.

Kris and Sarah Atkinson

"Sweet Tea" needed a lot more than sugar to be the Southern beauty she is today. Sixty years ago, the original owners bought the little aluminum trailer to store pig feed so critters couldn't get to it. They aptly nicknamed her the "Pig Camper." After all that time in the hot, humid Texas weather, a whole lot more than critters had taken its toll on the ten-foot vintage camper trailer.

In 2013, Kris and Sarah Atkinson acquired the little trailer and decided to give it a new lease on life. They found holes where the rats had chewed through the flooring and sides, and when they removed the aluminum from the outside, the whole structure literally fell apart in a heap. This may have scared some builders away, but not Kris and Sarah. Using his AutoCAD degree, Kris was able to create a design for their tiny trailer restoration.

After falling in love with the classic design of the teardrop, which typically sleeps only two, they needed to make some big changes. This amazing custom birchwood teardrop was designed to meet the exact needs of the Atkinson family, and comfortably sleeps the four of them as well as their two dogs.

In six months the frame-to-finish restoration was complete. Now the Atkinsons enjoy taking their trailer to vintage camper rallies and on family camping trips. Each year, Kris and Sarah and their two daughters, Hannah and Kayla, spend their vacation time camping by the river. Everywhere they go, Sweet Tea turns heads, and Sarah said she never tires of showing off her husband's craftsmanship. This once-canned-ham-turned-custom-teardrop is now an integral part of the wonderful memories they continue to make together as a family.

THIS PAGE AND FACING: The "Pig Camper" is transformed into "Sweet Tea."

The Atkinsons' teardrop could be the largest custom-made teardrop ever made. It sleeps four (plus two dogs) and has its own mini-fridge. All photos on pages 102-03 by Sarah Atkinson, except photo at right by Lauren Victoria/Lauren Victoria Photography.

All photos on pages 104-05 by Lauren Victoria/LaurenVictoria Photography.

ABOVE: **Mariana McElroy-Cook, Levi Cook, and David Cook (left to right). All photos this page submitted by Mariana McElroy-Cook.**

Mariana McElroy-Cook

Mariana McElroy-Cook, from Wasaga Beach, Ontario, said that she follows the Vintage Camper Trailers Facebook page and considers herself a glamper. This is "Vera," her 1961 Glendale Glendette. She is sixteen feet long, including bumper and hitch, and was made in Strathroy, Ontario. The Cooks use her for camping, as a mobile vintage pop-up shop, and starting in 2016, for event rentals.

Brian and Paul Geary

Twin brothers Brian and Paul Geary from Southern California are genuine gearheads. They have spent their entire lives building, rebuilding, manufacturing, tuning, changing, and upgrading everything that has wheels. Paul and Brian chuckled as they recalled building lawn mowers and Soap Box Derby cars as kids. Everything was going well until they passed their mom while going fifty-six miles per hour down a hill in their souped-up push car. In high school, they worked at Orange County Raceway after it opened. They shared stories of racing legends giving them parts and helping the brothers work on their projects.

Brian and his wife, Cathy, live in Big Bear, California and have quite a collection of fun trailers. In 1975, they bought a 1955 Fagoul Twin Coach that was used to deliver batteries for Goodyear

Brian Geary and his wife, Cathy, converted this 1955 Fagoul Twin Coach into a camper.

Tires. Brian rebuilt the Twin Coach into a motor home. He finished it in 1980 and used it for a couple of years before it sat unused until 2013. He and Cathy decided to revamp it in 2014, and enjoyed the fruits of their hard work at the vintage trailer rally at Lighthouse RV Park in Big Bear. They also enjoy their 1947 Travelite, and are looking forward to redoing their Royal Spartanette that brother Paul bought in Huntington Beach, California, to match Paul and wife Donna's Spartanette (it's a twin thing). Cathy is instrumental in organizing the Pismo South Vintage Camper

Trailer Rally at Campland on the Bay in San Diego during the month of April, and helps Brian with the decorating and restoration of their trailers.

When Paul and Donna decided they wanted a vintage trailer to take camping, naturally they let Brian and Cathy know what they were looking for. In 2006, Brian found them a thirty-foot, tandem-axle 1951 Spartanette in Big Bear. It was sitting on the side of a hill, *full* of stuff. It had been lived in for thirty-five years. After checking the wheels and bearings, they towed it to their home in Tustin, California (which they call Spartan Central), and used the next year to restore it. In true Geary fashion, the trailer is a beautiful piece of artwork, with fun upgrades like their dinette that is built out of steel. Donna has done a striking job beautifying the Spartan with period-correct decorations and fabrics. The Geary brothers and their wives are some of the real characters who make this hobby so fun and enjoyable.

THIS PAGE AND FACING: Paul and Donna Geary's thirty-foot 1951 Spartanette.

The Couples

From tackling restoration challenges as a team to relaxing together by a campfire, couples enjoy the hobby of vintage camper trailering. From empty nesters to retirees to weekend warriors, these couples have found a place to belong. Many share stories of how the hobby has given them something fun to do together and strengthened their relationships.

FACING: **Dan and Susan Cutright and their Traveleze trailer (see page 127).**

Lara and Leif Berglund

Following a once-in-a-lifetime trip to Hawaii, Lara and her previous husband decided that they would like to travel more, even if they couldn't afford the luxury of Hawaii on a regular basis. They found a twenty-four-foot 1965 Airstream Tradewind that they fixed up and enjoyed. After her husband passed away in 2003, Lara sold the Airstream—but she really missed camping.

So when Lara and Leif Berglund began dating, they decided to rebuild a vintage trailer. To the novice eye, Lara and Leif seemed to have found a perfect trailer. However, they soon realized that their 1965 Avion was a bit more than they felt comfortable tackling

The Berglunds' 1965 Avion Sportsman 21.

as their first restoration project. To prepare, they decided to become restoration experts while rebuilding a 1960 Mobile Scout. Once the Mobile Scout was restored, the Berglunds found that they really enjoyed talking with people about their vintage trailer.

They then entered what Lara described as their hoarding phase, and had soon gathered five more trailers. Completing the easier restoration on the Mobile Scout, Leif and Lara felt more equipped to take on the Avion's spongy floors, leaks, water damage, and mold.

"It was rough, very rough," said Lara as she chuckled and shook her head.

In 2012, the Berglunds were ready to take their Avion Sportsman 21 on its maiden voyage. Just one mile down the road the door flew open. Upon inspection, Leif and Lara found no curve in the door where it had previously been curved to match the trailer. They turned around, switched trailers, and continued to their destination.

Later they replaced the door and took the Avion to its first rally in Lynden, Washington. Like so many other trailerites, Leif and Lara said they felt like they had found their tribe after attending their first rally. Now they, along with their dog, June Bug, enjoy attending and helping at vintage camper trailer rallies.

LEFT: June Bug sunning herself on the once spongy floor of Lara and Leif Berglund's 1965 Avion Sportsman 21. ABOVE AND BELOW: The interior of the Avion.

Jeff and Nanci Hill

trailer built for two. With five grandchildren, they have recently acquired another vintage trailer (a 1965 Barth) that sleeps four, so they can start taking extras on their camping adventures.

Jeff and Nanci Hill and their 1957 Arrowhead.

Jeff and Nanci Hill, parents of seven grown children, were looking for a car for their daughter when they picked up a copy of *Auto Trader* in 2005. At the back of the magazine were two cute trailers for sale. On a whim, they bought their 1957 Arrowhead from the second owner, who had purchased it from the original owner six months earlier. The original owner had purchased the trailer, taken his family camping once to Pismo Beach, California, and then parked it in covered storage. After promising the owner that they would use the trailer for camping, the Hills became the new owners.

Not knowing anything about the vintage camper trailer hobby, the Hills enjoyed dry camping for five years before they found out about rallies. The interior of the Arrowhead is all original except for the curtains. Until 2012, the exterior was original as well, but after running over a tire on the freeway, the front passenger side of the Arrowhead was smashed. They fixed the damage and had it repainted avocado green and 1960 Ford white. Jeff, a UPS driver, and Nanci, a retired law clerk, have enjoyed their

Robert and Carolyn Engstrom

ABOVE: Robert and Carolyn Engstrom in front of their "Lounge a-Go-Go." BELOW: The interior of Go-Go is luxuriously appointed. Photos by Ernesto Rivera/Chico News and Review.

Robert and Carolyn Engstrom spent many a night tent camping while raising their six children. After their children grew up and moved out, the Engstroms were done with tents, but not with camping. Taking inspiration from Robert's father's retirement dream of traveling the country in a vintage trailer, they began their search for the perfect vessel. Searching online ultimately led them to an intriguing trailer, and an intriguing idea.

The Engstroms fell for a 1962 Avalair that was still mostly original on the outside, but had been renovated inside as a lounge! She now sported seating for twelve, a fridge, and a wine cooler. However, she still had the capacity to hold a double bed. The trailer was the perfect blend of old-fashioned and newfangled. Seeing her in person sparked an idea. Not only was she right for the Engstroms, but also as a mobile event lounge. Through this vision, "Lounge a-Go-Go" was born.

Robert and Carolyn spent the fall of 2013 untangling all the ins and outs of launching a new business and getting Go-Go outfitted with a spanking new heating/air-conditioning unit. In January 2014, she made her debut at a local bridal show. So far, Lounge a-Go-Go has attended numerous weddings and club meetings, a baby shower, and a housewarming, and has been a VIP lounge at a concert. The Engstroms are looking forward to many more adventures with their Go-Go, and can't wait to play a part in other people's important days.

Dave and Sandy Loewen

The Loewens use their immaculately maintained 1965 Ford pickup to tow their 1959 Mercury trailer.

Dave and Sandy Loewen have a strong appreciation for history. As the third generation to live in their ancestral home, they understand the importance of family roots and keeping things in good shape for future generations to enjoy.

Dave has been a car guy forever. He bought his '65 Ford truck in 1983 and has carefully maintained its originality. The truck still has its original paint and interior. In 2008, after attending a car show that had vintage camper trailers, Dave and Sandy bought a 1959 Mercury camper trailer. A self-proclaimed Ford guy, Dave said that he had to buy the Mercury when he heard its name. Camp-ready, the only work the Mercury needed was a vintage-inspired wooden screen door built by Sandy's brother.

Dave was approached by a friend about a bike that he had been commissioned to sell. Dave ended up buying the 1951 Monarch bicycle from the original owner. The original owner was a young boy during World War II. As Japanese Americans, he and his family had been sent to an internment camp. After being allowed to return home, the father of the young boy spent his first paycheck buying that bicycle for his son. Now, Dave and Sandy are happy to use this bicycle and tell its story.

The Loewens enjoy towing their vintage camper trailer with their original Ford truck to attend rallies and car shows. They both agreed that the truck and trailer were the reason they got into the hobby. However, the people and the community of trailerites are what keep them coming back.

Dave and Sandy Loewen had to do very little work on their camp-ready 1959 Mercury.

Chuck and Denise Collier

Chuck and Denise Collier inherited Chuck's grandparents' 1967 Ford Country Sedan station wagon, and decided they would like to have a vintage trailer to tow behind their wagon. In 2010 they found a seventeen-foot 1963 Traveleze for sale on Craigslist. They spent the first year fixing up "Willma" and making her roadworthy. Denise felt the trailer was a "fabulous idea," as Chuck had discussed buying a boat. During the first year of restoration life became busy, and at one point Chuck almost sold the trailer because the projects were stacking up and he was feeling overwhelmed. Thankfully, Denise convinced them to take a moment and breathe, and they decided to continue on with the restoration. Now the Colliers enjoy camping in the beautiful Pacific Northwest with Willma and are "so in love with her." Chuck savors his satisfaction in saving a beautiful piece of history for the next generation to enjoy.

Chuck and Denise Collier restored this 1963 Traveleze trailer to tow behind their 1967 Ford Country Sedan station wagon. Above photo submitted by Chuck Collier.

Tim and Linda Brown

Tim Brown has camped in Yosemite at least once every other year for the past forty years. He hasn't missed a year for the past ten. A lifelong hot-rodder and builder, Tim has an appreciation for antiques and vintage.

While looking for a Mother's Day gift for his wife, Linda, it wasn't much of a stretch for him to look for a vintage camper trailer. He found a Corvette camper trailer for sale on Craigslist. Tim and Linda bought that little trailer on Mother's Day, 2006. Tim took it home and had it torn apart in twenty-four hours and lying in stacks in his yard. Linda simply looked at the heaps and reminded him that he had one year, not seven, to complete the project. Linda is always working with Tim to help finish whatever their latest project might be.

Using the original Corvette as a pattern, they did a total rebuild on their trailer. It was decorated in hot-rod style and painted black and silver. That little trailer started a new business for the Browns. As professional painters, they were hit hard when the economy floundered in 2008. The expertise that Tim and Linda gained by redoing their first trailer paid off. According to Tim, the shop classes, welding classes, and automotive classes taken in high school helped out too. The level of work that the Browns did on their own trailer soon had other trailerites commissioning them to restore their trailers. In the past nine years, the Browns have been responsible for repairing and restoring more than thirty vintage camper trailers. Several of Tim and Linda's restorations have graced the cover of issues of *Vintage Camper Trailers* magazine.

Authors' Note: We were the sellers of the Browns' first Corvette trailer. That Mother's Day transaction resulted in a special friendship that we still share with Tim and Linda to this day.

The curtains, quilt, and canopy on this 1959 DeVille trailer showcase Linda's skills as a seamstress.

Rob and Jolaine Collins

Rock-and-roll music has been a part of Rob and Jolaine Collins' relationship since they dated in the '70s. Both of them grew up listening to music by the Beatles, Jimi Hendrix, and Janis Joplin, and their diverse musical tastes are heard in the couple's album collection.

So it's fitting that their 1961 Kencraft trailer is an homage to the music of the '60s and named "Li'l Woodstock." Framed concert posters, a lava lamp, and a record player spinning a variety of tunes are reminiscent of the golden age of rock and roll.

"We tried to imagine how it would have been, traveling in the '60s with a trailer and enjoying the era's evolving music scene. Our trailer wardrobe includes plenty of paisley, tie-dye, and fringed leather," said Jolaine, whose career in public relations includes presenting themed events. A graphic designer, Rob created much of the art in the trailer using iconic images of musicians from the '60s.

The Kencraft's original, refurbished interior is striking, with its lustrous birchwood paneling, large windows, and rear door, which create a feeling of openness. Bark cloth curtains and banquette seats that convert to a king-size bed make it extra cozy.

The couple purchased their Kencraft in 2009 at the suggestion of a vintage car–collecting friend who'd just purchased a rare Shasta model. Together they shared the experiences of refurbishing their first trailers and traveling to vintage camper rallies.

Vintage trailer camping seems like a natural progression for Rob and Jolaine, who enjoyed many years of backpacking and tent camping throughout California and Colorado before deciding it was much more comfortable sleeping on a king-size camper bed than the hard ground.

Rob and Jolaine Collins and their rock-and-roll-inspired 1961 Kencraft.

Crit and Jennifer Rivera

Watching Crit and Jennifer Rivera relaxing in front of their 1970 Kencraft, you would never know that they almost didn't make it in the camping hobby. Crit recalled that some of his best memories growing up were the times he spent camping with his parents in their late-1950s Traveleze. His grandparents owned a nearby campground, but Crit and his parents camped elsewhere because dogs were not allowed at his grandparents' establishment.

Fast-forward twenty years and Crit is married with two young children. Desiring to share the happiness he had experienced while camping with his children, the family dived into the camping world. After three failed camping trips (including blown transmissions, drunks circling their camper at 2 a.m. on ATVs, being rained out, trains going by, helicopters circling, and parking their trailer in fish goo), Jennifer recalls grabbing Crit with two hands in the middle of the night and declaring that was the end of their camping adventures.

Crit decided to sneak in one last camping trip with his kids, Lilly and Ellis, before selling the camper. They had a fantastic time singing and dancing by a fire, and came back to tell Jennifer all about their fun. Jennifer acquiesced and agreed to go on another outing. It turned out to be delightful, so they took their trailer off the market and camped in it for several years.

After searching on Craigslist for almost a year, they found their

ABOVE AND BELOW: **The Kencraft as it would have looked in 1970.**

1970 Kencraft. It had been stored indoors for more than thirty years. Crit asked the original owner what needed to be restored on the trailer. The owner suggested that the butter dish in the fridge may need to be replaced because it had a crack in it. Crit knew from that answer that he had found an original jewel. The Rivera family now enjoys camping in luxury in their like-new 1970 Kencraft.

Dan and Susan Cutright

Sitting by the fire and sipping a glass of wine in front of their 1954 Traveleze trailer is Dan and Susan Cutright's favorite part of camping. They enjoy the social aspect of the hobby and the friends they have made at the rallies. As a member of the board of Napa County Landmarks, a nonprofit dedicated to the preservation of historic buildings in Napa County, California, Dan wants to see historical sites maintained for the next generations to enjoy. He also has a passion for preserving vintage trailers.

Dan recalls camping most summers during the 1960s. He and his family camped at a classic campground in Guerneville, California. Those great memories are ones that Dan and Susan wanted to create with their own family. While determining what avenue to pursue to get back into camping, Dan found his first fifteen-foot Traveleze in 1999. Dan hired Craig Dorsey to restore

this trailer, which was Craig's first trailer restoration completed on contract. Dan and Susan had their trailer back and ready for camping six months later.

While the Cutrights really enjoyed their first Traveleze, they wanted to upgrade to a trailer with a bathroom. When they found their twenty-one-foot Traveleze with a bathroom, they started the restoration process all over again. Their trailer is now fully self-contained and wired with twelve volts and cable.

Dan and Susan enjoy their vintage trailer, and often have their children and grandchildren with them when they are camping. They had a full awning room added to the trailer so the kids have a place to sleep. They are now busy working on making many more memories as a family and preserving a piece of midcentury America.

Daniel and Bernie Donovan

Eighteen-year veterans of the vintage camper trailer hobby, Daniel and Bernie Donovan know a rare trailer when they spot it. After being in the hobby for so many years, people knew whom to call when they saw a trailer for sale. In October 2013, an ad for a 1936 Covered Wagon was placed on Craigslist in New Hampshire. Tin Can Tourists reposted it to their website. A friend of a friend posted it to Facebook. Seeing the trailer on Facebook, another friend called her husband, who then called Daniel. Daniel got the call at 9 p.m. Pacific Standard Time, and immediately called the seller in New Hampshire—midnight their time! A quick conversation set up a phone call for the next morning, when Daniel said he would buy the trailer.

Daniel and his brother Michael, a long-time finishing carpenter, furniture builder, and trailer restorer, set off for a nine-day road trip to New Hampshire to pick up their new acquisition. They replaced the tires, repacked the bearings, shrink-wrapped the trailer, and drove through snowstorms in the Chicago area before making it to California on its own wheels.

The trailer was originally purchased by A. F. Lemieux, who used his '36 Chevy to tow it home. He was a postal worker on the railroad. He would deliver mail to towns along his route and sleep in the trailer at the end of his day. When he retired, it was

Bernie and Daniel Donovan and their incredibly rare 1936 Covered Wagon.

The Donovans have done a meticulous restoration of their 1936 Covered Wagon trailer.

stored for thirty years in a garage. It was then moved to a shed and suffered snow damage when the shed collapsed during a storm. It was last used in 1972 for hunting.

When Daniel and Michael got it home, Daniel's wife, Bernie, rebuilt the couch and made new curtains for the inside. They plan to leave the rest of the interior in original condition. They are in the process of restoring the exterior with help from Michael.

At this time, only one other 1936 Covered Wagon Master model is known to exist.

The Donovans, like Mr. Lemieux, plan on towing the 1936 Covered Wagon with their 1936 Chevy Master Deluxe.

Faye and Barry Holland

When Barry and Faye Holland retired, they decided they needed a project to work on together. A shared venture would allow them to get reacquainted after years of raising children and careers. A trip to the Harley shop soon eliminated motorcycles as their new hobby; although enthusiastic about the possibility, the reality of jumping on and off the bike was more than they wanted to attempt. Their next idea was a new camper trailer. After looking at new trailers, Faye was so disappointed in the interior décor, she recalls telling the sales lady that she would have to redo the whole trailer. Barry decided looking for an older trailer and fixing it up might be the right idea for a project they could do together. While visiting with a neighbor, he mentioned his idea and the neighbor told him he knew where a vintage camper trailer might be for sale. What they went to see was a barn-fresh 1959 Boles Aero in mint condition. Unfortunately, after months of back and forth with the owner, he decided not to sell. The Hollands were now hooked on the idea of a vintage trailer and went on the search. Each time a trailer came up for sale, they would be fourth or fifth in line to look at it.

They found a 1964 Shasta Compact, and after calling about it, were fourth in line to see the trailer. Barry asked the owner to please keep his number and call if the first three buyers fell through. Unexpectedly, a week later the owner called and said the trailer was still for sale. Barry recalled the seller asking him tons of

questions. When they went to see the trailer they found the three previous potential buyers had not met the seller's requirements. One wanted to turn it into a hot dog stand, one a taco stand, and the third a rolling brothel. Faye and Barry quickly realized they were being interviewed for ownership. They passed the test and bought their first vintage trailer.

As they began the fix-up, it became apparent they were better off to gut it and start over. Barry and Faye were worried the neighbors might be upset by the vintage trailer in the driveway, but it was just the opposite. Neighbors and passersby would stop for visits, sharing their camping tales as they checked in on the Hollands' progress. Almost weekly they would find a little gift (camping related) on the table of the Shasta with a card of well wishes. Six months later, they were just finishing their renovation the night before their first rally, but they made it!

Dubbed the "Vintage Camper Evangelists," Faye and Barry are always meeting new people, sharing their love of vintage trailers, and making converts. Faye said that she and Barry agree that vintage camper trailering has been one of the best things they have done in their forty-seven-year marriage, second only to raising their boys, Bryan and Michael.

Wayne and Kathy Ferguson

Wayne Ferguson's love of vintage trailers goes back to his early childhood. If he was a "good boy," he would get to take his naps in his grandparents' Mercury trailer. Those trailer naps instilled a lifelong appreciation for the wood, warmth, and coziness of '50s-era trailers. Wayne first began restoring vintage trailers for his family's use in the early 1980s. He wanted his children to share the experience he had as a youngster. Over time, Wayne became captivated by all things vintage trailer and developed into a self-taught trailer historian, collecting trailer literature and learning all he could about the history of trailer building in the United States and abroad.

Kathy Ferguson loved camping, hiking, and the outdoors from an early age. Her family camped at the beach every summer; she was a Girl Scout and later a summer camp counselor. Kathy grew up in a family of do-it-yourselfers. Her father was never afraid to tackle any household renovation or build whatever project he needed, and her mother encouraged and taught Kathy to sew, paint, and refinish furniture.

That combination has made for a great partnership—not only in marriage, but also in trailer restoration. Wayne restores the electrical, mechanical, plumbing, appliances, and structure of the trailers; he is so proficient that he can do it with his eyes closed—literally! Wayne has been legally blind since the mid-1980s. He continues to lose his eyesight, but not his enthusiasm for the vintage trailer hobby and for working on vintage trailers. Kathy's contributions to the restoration process are the finishes and décor. She brings the interior wood and floor back to life, sews drapes and curtains, and enjoys searching for vintage pieces to make the Fergusons' camping trailer a home away from home.

Hal and Marilyn Thoms

Can you imagine six-foot-five Hal Thoms fitting into and enjoying a thirteen-foot Aljoa trailer? He does! Through a series of serendipitous events, Hal and Marilyn Thoms have found their element in the vintage camper trailer hobby. In 2013 they watched some neighbors transform a dilapidated camper trailer into a restored masterpiece. Both Hal and Marilyn enjoyed checking his progress each day as they drove past.

As publisher of 356 *Club* magazine and a professional auto photographer, Hal is no stranger to the world of vintage vehicles. When the Thomses saw a second vintage trailer parked in the yard down the street, they decided to meet their neighbors, John and Connie Palmer. The Palmers had restored their 1953 Aljoa to take camping and rallying. The Palmers needed a slightly larger trailer, and so they were going to sell their Aljoa after they had

BELOW: **Hal and Marilyn Thoms go everywhere in their 1953 Aljoa and 1961 Studebaker Champ pickup. Photos on pages 134-35 by Hal Thoms.**

restored that second trailer. Hal and Marilyn looked at the little trailer and fell in love. After Hal tried out the bed and fit, the Thomses knew this trailer was meant for them. They bought it from the Palmers right then and there.

After attending their first rally, they decided that their special trailer warranted a period-correct tow rig. A 1961 Studebaker Champ that had been in the same family for more than forty years was found, and the Thomses are now enjoying their ensemble, taking them on camping trips two or three times a month.

Jim and Shelley Luke

Jim and Shelley Luke are traditional hot-rodders. In the fall of 2009, they and several of their hot-rodder friends took their cars on a Saturday afternoon drive to a vintage camper trailer rally. Shelley said, "We went as spectators, and as soon as we saw those little gems, we knew we had to get a trailer and be a part of the fun."

Then in February 2010, Shelley was diagnosed with leukemia. The Lukes' plans to buy and fix up a vintage camper trailer were put on hold. While Shelley was going through chemo and a subsequent stem cell transplant at an out-of-state clinic, their friend Tim Brown helped the Lukes acquire a 1958 Corvette trailer. While Shelley was recovering

ABOVE AND FACING, BOTTOM RIGHT: **Interior shots of Jim and Shelly Luke's 1959 Corvette trailer.**

from her transplant, Jim was back at home with their teenage son, Jake, who was finishing high school. During that time, Jim and Tim worked to restore the trailer. Shelley said, "Jim would send me pictures of the progress each night to give me something to look forward to."

Shelley's stem cell transplant worked. The leukemia was gone, but it managed to destroy her kidneys. Shelley was able to return home in April 2011. Her new schedule was three days a week of painful dialysis sessions. Being on dialysis means you are unable to do anything spontaneously. Everything needs to be planned weeks in advance if you want to travel. Being able to make little weekend trips in their vintage trailer was a wonderful getaway for the family. Shelley would go to dialysis early on a Friday morning so they could leave on a Friday afternoon and enjoy their weekend. Jim and Shelley made their first camping trip in the fall of 2011. They went to the same place they had gone as spectators two years earlier.

For three and a half years, the Lukes have been able to go to many local vintage trailer rallies. They have become friends with great people. In early 2015, Linda Brown, wife of Tim Brown, found out that she and Shelley were the same blood type. While attending a burger night with trailer friends, Linda told Shelley she was in the process of being tested in an attempt to be a living donor. However, on May 8, 2015, Shelley got the call that a kidney had been found for her. She had a kidney transplant the next morning. The Lukes had planned to go camping at Pismo Beach, but that trip had to be cancelled while Shelley recovered from her transplant.

Jim and Shelley are looking forward to being able to now go to vintage camper trailer rallies without having to schedule dialysis, and without the food restrictions associated with kidney disease. For several years Shelley has been unable to eat the delicious cupcakes that Linda usually takes to rallies—but not anymore! As Shelley said, "Life is good!

ABOVE: **Shelley with friends Tim and Linda Brown (see page 120).**

Jimmy and Michelle Proctor

Jimmy and Michelle Proctor are the kind of people who make this hobby so special. As owners of a body and paint shop in California, they have the skills necessary to make vintage camper trailers shine. Jimmy was doing just that when he met a longtime collector of vintage camper trailers. Jimmy and Michelle bought their 1956 Rod and Reel from him. As collectors and lovers of old things, Jimmy said he "was born thirty years too late." The Proctors were using their trailer to go camping and hang out with friends long before they realized there was such a thing as rallies. Now they enjoy attending several rallies a year.

Steve and Terry Mendenhall

Heads turn when Steve and Terry Mendenhall are seen traveling down the highway in a beautifully restored 1955 Chevy Bel Air convertible towing a 1955 Boles Aero Mira Mar—a match made in heaven! Much like the car and trailer, Steve and Terry are an incredible couple. Preparing to celebrate their thirty-sixth anniversary, they chuckle at the fact that they can still be so engrossed in each other and their conversation that they miss highway turn-offs. They have started reminding each other not to chat as they are getting close to where they need to exit.

A retired mechanic for a Caterpillar dealership, Steve is a wonder-worker with all things mechanical. As a longtime car guy, Steve was just twenty-four years old when he first saw a hot rod towing a trailer. From that time on, Steve wanted a trailer to tow. In January 2007, the Mendenhalls found a '56 Airstream Bubble for sale in the *Goodguys Goodtimes Gazette* magazine.

They purchased the trailer out of Arizona and enjoyed camping in her for two years.

In 2007, they saw a 1955 Boles Aero at a campout—the original owners were still enjoying it! Steve and Terry were able to tour it, and when it came up for sale six months later they knew it was the trailer they wanted. They are overjoyed with the flushing toilet in that little trailer! How much luckier could they be?

Not only do Steve and Terry enjoy camping with their vintage trailers and restoring old cars, they also have a wool ranch where they show and breed around 120 award-winning Merino ewes. Even with all their hobbies, Terry still enjoys her part-time work as a neonatal intensive care nurse. While Terry is working, Steve is busy on their next project: a 1952 Chevy panel truck to tow their "new" twenty-nine-foot 1954 Boles Aero Estrellita.

Nick Uribe and Laura Waterhouse

Avid athletes and outdoors people, Nick Uribe and Laura Waterhouse were looking for a way to enjoy the great outdoors but get up off the ground and into a comfy bed. This dangerous thought led to looking on the Internet, where they found pictures of vintage camper trailers. They then bid on and won a 1965 Drifter located in Palm Springs, California, in an eBay auction. A day's drive from their home, Nick and Laura planned an entire vacation around picking up their new acquisition. They arrived to pick up their Drifter as newbies to the vintage camper trailers hobby.

They enjoyed camping in their trailer on their way home, and took the Drifter to a few campouts before Nick suggested replacing the water-damaged wood. One piece of rot led to another and soon the entire trailer was in pieces. After four years of trying to remodel the Drifter, it found its final resting home at the local landfill. The most expensive candelabra at one of the Tin Can Tourists' events was made out of the license plate and various parts from the defunct Drifter.

Nick and Laura's shaky start with vintage didn't deter them from looking for another vintage camper trailer. They found their second trailer through eBay as well. It just happened to be the first trailer that *we* ever sold. Nick and

Laura showed up at our home leery of the description, but thankfully the 1968 Shasta Loflyte with mint green interior was as described and a deal was made. A long-lasting friendship was born between us and Nick and Laura.

The '68 Shasta is Laura's special place, a place to decorate and hide out. Nick replaced the floor on the day they were to attend their very first rally. As Laura was packing up to go, Nick came into the house with a cut on his thumb. He insisted he was okay and that they should continue on to the rally. Laura convinced him to stop at the emergency room. A few stitches later and several hours late, they arrived at their first rally.

While they loved their '68 Shasta Loflyte, Nick wanted a trailer with a bathroom. Their third trailer was also found on eBay—a 1967 Shasta Starflyte. They now primarily use the '67 Starflyte to camp and have set up a "campground" in their front yard for their '68 Shasta Loflyte to serve as a guest home. Nick loves the simple life of camping so much he is trying to convince Laura to sell everything and live in their vintage trailers. Laura also loves the camping life, and as president of the NorCal chapter of the Tow Girlz Vintage Camper Trailers Club, she shares this love with anyone who shows interest in the hobby.

Gary and Sally Lodholm

While attending an antique show, Gary and Sally Lodholm spotted a pair of Shasta wings peeking out behind some brush. The retired couple stopped to inquire, and soon owned their first vintage camper trailer. With nothing to do in their early retirement, the couple took on the restoration project with gusto. Gary said that with their basic skills they were able to completely restore the Shasta. Now the Lodholms continue to collect and restore vintage camper trailers. Sally said they just restore and collect, but never sell. They are on vintage camper trailer number five!

The Lodholms have particularly enjoyed meeting the original owners of the trailers they rescue. Their 1947 Westwood was purchased from Marion, a ninety-eight-year-old widow living on the coastal shores of Washington State. It took the Lodholms a year and a half to build a relationship with Marion in order for her to sell them "her baby." Marion and her husband, Lawrence, special ordered the Westwood in 1947. While the trailer was being built, Lawrence would check on its progress daily. Lawrence's attention to detail allowed this trailer to survive on the coast for over sixty years because he insisted that the window frames be made out of aluminum.

When the Lodholms were able to purchase the Westwood, for the same $2,500 price that Marion and Lawrence had paid in 1947, it was a mess. It took

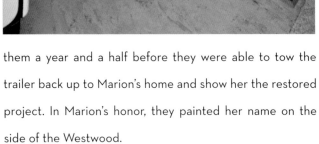

them a year and a half before they were able to tow the trailer back up to Marion's home and show her the restored project. In Marion's honor, they painted her name on the side of the Westwood.

Gary said it is the "best fun" to once again share their restored trailers with the original owners and see the appreciation for preserving something that had meant so much to them. The Lodholms continue to enjoy the restoration process of vintage camper trailers, as well as attending rallies and camping with family.

John and Connie Palmer

A retired sales manager, John Palmer was asked by his son to build him a teardrop that he could park in his limited garage space. After building that teardrop, he built several more before moving on to small stand-up trailers. His first canned ham rebuild was on a 1953 Aljoa, which now belongs to John and Connie's neighbors, Hal and Marilyn Thoms (see page 134).

Living on a busy street, the Palmers have had several of their neighbors stop to see what John was working on in his driveway. Now they are camping with many of those neighbors in vintage camper trailers, some of which John has helped rebuild.

John is a true craftsman who loves to restore these trailers from the ground up. He is retired, so he only takes on projects that he thinks look fun and interesting. His focus is on restoring vintage trailers to better-than-new condition. Because these trailers are camped in frequently, modern amenities are added, but hidden so the trailer keeps the vintage feel. Connie is the "curtain person," sewing the curtains for the finished trailers.

John and most of his vintage trailer friends started out as car guys. With wives who were burnt out on attending car shows, the vintage camper trailer rallies allow both partners to enjoy their weekends. John and the guys can still show their cars and tinker with trailers, but most importantly the wives can enjoy decorating their campers and visiting with their friends. John and Connie are excited about their current and future restoration projects.

Craig and Diana Thomas's 1951 Spartenette Tandem.

Craig and Diana Thomas

The vintage camper trailer hobby started for Craig Thomas and his wife, Diana, when they purchased a 1956 Airstream Flying Cloud. It was only a shell, yet Diana was excited about the possibilities of fixing it. At about the same time, they found a twenty-seven-foot 1951 Spartanette Tandem. Craig instantly was drawn to the Spartanette, as he recalled spending time in one as a child in the mountains of New Mexico. With the emotional connection to the Spartanette, the Thomas family decided to restore it prior to the Flying Cloud. This was going to be a huge endeavor, as the Spartanette needed a full restoration.

Craig, a visual effects artist, knew very little about restoration, but was willing to learn. He used the Internet to guide his learning and watched a lot of YouTube to acquire the restoration skills necessary to complete the process. Craig mentioned that restoring a trailer requires mastering several different skills, but they can all be accomplished.

It has taken the Thomases three years to restore the Spartanette. They completely gutted the interior to the aluminum exterior. They installed all-new electrical, plumbing, and insulation, replaced all of the wood paneling, and laser-cut wood details throughout. Visually the trailer looks completely vintage, but Craig has used his design background to hide all the necessary items to make the trailer totally modern. This includes a "control center" created from an antique shortwave radio, which acts as the central sound system. Plus there is a hidden HVAC system and discretely placed LED lights throughout.

With the couple's common interest in antiques, the vintage camper trailer hobby was a natural progression for them. Diana, the vice president for a health and fitness company, has a dream of sharing their restored vintage camper trailers through Airbnb. They are well on their way to realizing this dream, as they have a few trailers already collected and restored. Craig and Diana have enjoyed the gratification that comes from sharing something that they have poured their heart and souls into—making something classic usable once again

The Thomases' trailer is completely rebuilt with custom woodwork and all the latest gadgets.

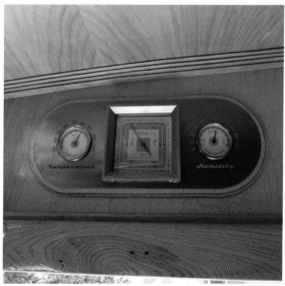

Photos on pages 150–51 by Jen Sawn.

Frank and Tamitha Lewis

It's hard to know which came first, the trailer or the dream. Frank and Tamitha Lewis always had RVs, but one day decided they wanted an Airstream. In 2009, they purchased a custom 1977 Airstream Safari with the Wally Byam Caravan Club number 47. As it turned out, their encounter with the Airstream was short lived. While they loved the outside, they hated all of the plastic materials used in the impeccable "all-original" interior and couldn't bear to change it. The Lewises only owned it for a month and sold it for almost twice what they paid for it. It was not their intention to flip the trailer, but it was intriguing.

Tamitha was fascinated with Sisters on the Fly and photos of their vintage trailer caravan trips. Tamitha knew that she would have her own little vintage trailer and would tow it all by herself. One day she ran across a local Northern California group called the Trailerettes. She immediately joined even though she did not have a trailer and had no towing experience. What she did have was a husband, Frank, who wanted her to realize her dream. So together they ignited an online pursuit that led to them driving twelve hours to purchase an unrestored 1965 Cardinal Lovebird with a ten-foot box. Initially, Frank would come and drop Tamitha off at her campsite and help her set up. It became affectionately referred to as the "Concierge Service" by her fellow Trailerettes. Eventually, Tamitha got her own tow vehicle, and Frank taught her how to tow and gave her the confidence to do it. Tamitha shared that "following this dream is one of the best things I've ever done for myself."

Frank and Tamitha caught a severe case of "Aluminitus." It's highly contagious and apparently there is no cure. Now they have a hobby that they enjoy together and individually. Their journey has been quite an evolution. They've had many trailers and the good intentions of restoring them, but ultimately realized that they could spend their time camping or they could spend their time restoring. The Lewises like to camp, so they've sent most of those trailers down the road and now are much more discriminating in their purchases. They prefer trailers that have been well cared for in "original" condition. For them, the vintage era is the appeal. It is fun for Tamitha to accessorize the trailers with period-appropriate items and bark cloth. Frank and Tamitha feel that these original vintage trailers are the closest thing they will probably ever experience to time travel. They are instantly transported to an idealistic time that inherently invites them to slow down and enjoy the simpler things in life. Tamitha said, "It's absolutely true—they don't make them like they used to!"

Frank and Tamitha's 1959 Streamline is their biggest trailer dream come true. They are still pinching themselves. They toured this trailer a couple of years ago at a rally and both absolutely fell in love with it. While attending another rally they found out the original Streamline was for sale. While not exactly in the market for another trailer, they felt that they could not let this one get away and became obsessed with making it happen. The trailer is a one-of-a-kind beauty inside and out. Frank and Tamitha are back in the silver trailer club, and hope to keep and enjoy their Streamline forever. They said that "regardless of which came first, this trailer is the dream!"

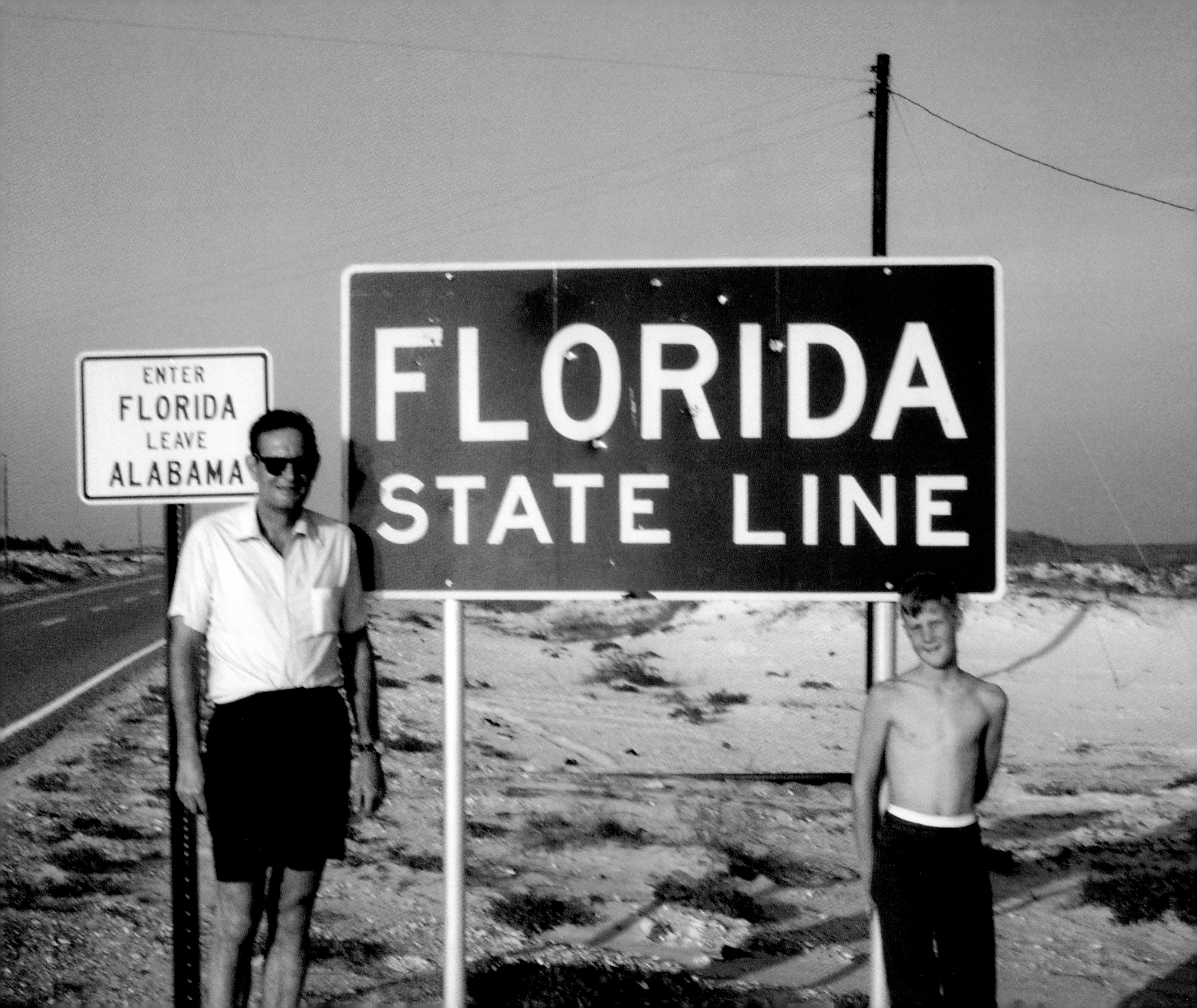
ENTER
FLORIDA
LEAVE
ALABAMA
FLORIDA
STATE LINE

The Lifers

The vintage trailer hobby has grown immensely in the past ten years. These folks, however, were already in the hobby well before then. They have been associated with vintage camper trailers, in some instances, before they were even "vintage"! Featured in this section are multigenerational families, friendships, and businesses that continue to contribute to the joy that the vintage camping revival brings to so many.

FACING: **John Carbett and his dad, Bill, stop for another picture as they enter Florida and leave Alabama (see page 160).**

Mary and Tony Alvarez / Joel and Rachel Harp

In 1962, Mary Alvarez was working for Pan Pacific Trailers at the end of the production line. She detailed camper trailers and let the builders know what was wrong before they were sent out to dealerships. After doing that job for a few years she went to work as a bookkeeper for an RV business. When her husband was facing layoffs at Aerojet in 1968, they decided that with Mary's experience in the industry, they should open an RV center. In 1969, KW RV Center in Citrus Heights, California, was opened. Mary and her family ran the business for thirty-six years.

Joel Harp came to work for Mary when he was just seventeen, and continued there for thirty-four years. He started by cleaning trailers. Mary said she had to get him young so she could train him up right for her daughter, Rachel. Joel married Rachel in 1972, and Rachel joined the family RV business in 1976 (after leaving her job at a bank that was robbed by Patty Hearst and the Symbionese Liberation Army).

They not only repaired and sold camper trailers, but they did specialty builds as well. Mary said she and Joel would sit together and brainstorm how

BELOW: **Tony and Mary Alvarez's Boles Aero towed by their 1968 Chevrolet Bel Air wagon. FACING: Tony and Mary Alvarez, Rachel and Joel Harp, and their son, Nicholas (left to right) posing in front of a Traveleze trailer.**

to make a customer's vision come to life. They built a mobile AIDS center, special vans that were used by the DMV to spy on potential lawbreakers, as well as manufactured conversion kits to convert a van to a camper. Joel even designed and built swamp coolers for the ASPCA's transport vehicles. The big box vans got too hot to be able to transport animals safely, so Joel figured out how to make a swamp cooler run off RV batteries. His design is still being used by the organization today.

KW RV Center was closed in 2005, and Mary retired with her husband, Tony, who had been doing the company books for more than twenty-five years. Joel and Rachel started their own business, Harp's RV Service. Rachel and Joel have been working together for more than forty years, are still married, and still loving what they do. Rachel said that they decided a long time ago that at 7 p.m. work was done. They do not talk shop until 8 a.m. the next morning. The third and fourth generations of the family have now joined the Harps in working in the RV industry. The Harps' son, Nicholas, helps Joel in

the shop, and their grandkids help with sweeping and cleaning. Rachel said she starts the kids out sweeping and moves them up to emptying holding tanks. She laughed when she said, "If they can handle that, they can handle just about anything."

Rachel has been writing articles and lecturing about how to RV safely since 1998. She primarily works with women who want to learn how to use their camper trailers. She teaches group classes as well as one-on-one sessions. She and Joel also host the Woodson Bridge Vintage Camper Rally each year in Corning, California. Several years ago they got a call from Jim and Betty Bradley saying they had a rare trailer that they would like them to take a look at. Jim brought the trailer in and showed it to Joel and Rachel. It turned out that the little European-made Sprite caravan was the same trailer that the Harps had used for their honeymoon forty years before. Now, each spring they get to see that little trailer at the rally and ask Jim and Betty if they are ready to sell that trailer back to them!

Larry Shank

Larry Shank's dad was always eager to see what lay over the next hill, but he had little time for paved roads. Armed with topographic maps and whatever folk wisdom he could gather from local guides, he preferred to find the next town by navigating stream beds or desolate plateaus—the more rugged the better. He usually had a fair idea of his current location but he wasn't given to sharing this fact with his family, leaving them to believe that he simply had a penchant for getting good and lost several times during each trip. This scared Larry's mom to death, but as a child Larry didn't know enough to be frightened. In his young eyes, this was just plain fun.

Back at home, his dad was an inveterate tinkerer who never stopped fine-tuning the family's workhorse, a Jeep CJ-3B. In late 1956, tired of second-gear slogs, he installed a 265-cubic-inch Chevrolet V-8, and along with his friends from Lockheed, where he worked as an engineer, designed and built a new engine/transmission adapter from scratch. Later modifications also included an engine-driven air compressor, eleven-inch brakes, a Warn overdrive, and a whole array of surplus aviation gauges. A variety of racks and mounts for carrying boats, extra fuel, and other sundries also accumulated over the years.

The family wanderings continued through one last trip with their complete Jeep-teardrop trailer combo in the 1980s. The CJ-3B, with Larry's dad at the wheel, remained a frequent sight around the streets of Glendale, California, but its age—and that of his dad and mom—spelled an end to its far-flung adventures.

Larry's parents continued to pull the teardrop behind their Oldsmobile wagon well into the early 1990s, and Larry and his wife, Pam, took them on one last trip with the trailer in 1992 (pulled behind Larry's 1984 Jeep Scrambler). By this time the Jeep CJ-3B and its Kenskill companion were easing into retirement.

Larry's mom and dad both passed in the early 2000s, but thanks to some rejuvenation, the CJ-3B and trailer are still going strong. Neither truck nor trailer will ever be 100 percent original or receive a frame-off restoration—his parents would have recoiled at the idea. It is, after all, the imperfections on this truck and trailer, what car folk refer to as *patina*, that tell the tale of their adventurous life with their family.

All photos this page submitted by Larry Shank.

John Carbett

John Carbett began his love affair with trailers when he was nine years old. It all started when his mom, Fran (picture Doris Day and Donna Reed rolled into one), wanted to bake a cake while camping. A family neighbor had a 1959 Shasta for sale, and when Fran walked in and saw the little oven, she soon had her husband, Bill, towing the trailer home. John still remembers the taste of that first chocolate cake baked in the trailer.

Two years later, John's parents hooked that Shasta up to their '64 Thunderbird and off they went on a three-month trip around the United States.

Bill had extended the tongue of the trailer to carry his Honda 50 and John's Schwinn ten-speed bicycle. That was one amazing rig! However, John, being a young boy, just wanted to stay in his neighborhood and play with his friends. That was the era when friends went out to play and came home when the streetlights came on, stopping play only long enough to gulp down peanut butter and jelly sandwiches and Kool-Aid. He just didn't understand why his nineteen-year-old brother got to stay home from the road trip.

However, John soon saw a bigger world outside his own backyard. There were kids to meet at every campsite; each campground was another opportunity to make new friends. The family made memories in the Shasta that summer, often sitting at a campfire bonding with new acquaintances. His mom's favorite saying about trailer life was, "If you don't like your neighbors, you can move!"

Every night, John and his dad would lie on the bed of the cozy trailer and mark out the route for the next day on a map that was taped on the bottom of John's upper bunk. When John's dad passed away at the age of ninety-three, thinking about planning those next-day adventures was—and always will be—a precious memory for John. No cell phone, no TV, no computer—just the two of them, being close and making memories.

All photos on pages 160-61 submitted by John Carbett.

John and his dad, Bill, posed before every state sign they passed. All photos submitted by John Carbett.

The trip was not *always* idyllic, however. Picture zigzagging thousands of miles in the small back seat of a Thunderbird while your dad smoked a cigar! No one thought about exposing kids to second-hand smoke or worried about easing the complaints of bothersome seatbelts by stuffing them between the seats.

The trailer gave priceless freedom. The family would wander along until they found the place they wanted to stay. Nowadays you'd better get online and get a reservation or you could end up in the Walmart parking lot!

On that trip, John and his family hit every state except South Dakota. A photo was taken of John next to the sign for each state entered. He now realizes how fortunate he was to see this truly beautiful country in this way. The trailer was their home on wheels for the summer. John's mom didn't lose her love for the little stove, and she was all about home-cooked meals in their little canned ham (even though that term didn't exist then).

Today, John and his wife, Jeanine (whom he met back in the original neighborhood he wasn't happy about leaving for a summer), have a 1957 Cardinal. They tow it behind a '64 Ford van and carry the same Honda 50 John's family took on their travels. The minute their family walks into the trailer, they go back to those simpler times. Even though they can "move if we don't like the neighbors" (as John's mother said), they have never had to do that, because they truly meet the nicest people while vintage camper trailering.

John and Jeanine Carbett pose with their 1957 Cardinal.

Steve Casagrande

Anne and A. E. Casagrande and their 1959 Shasta.

In 1959, Steve Casagrande's neighbors, Mary and Tom, bought a 1959 Shasta Airflyte. It was white on white and Steve's mother, Anne, loved it. Two weeks after Mary and Tom brought their trailer home, Tom and Steve's dad, A. E., were on their way back to the dealer in Bakersfield, California, to purchase the same identical Shasta for the Casagrande family.

A. E. and Anne Casagrande, a school teacher and homemaker, respectively, would take their five boys camping every summer. Steve said that their Shasta was well used and pretty trashed by the time the five boys were grown. He used it as his private study hall while attending dentistry school. Years later, Steve returned to the neighborhood where he was raised. Mary still had her Shasta and was more than willing to sell it to him. He spent the next eight months meticulously restoring the trailer. He painted the Shasta to match his original Chevy Bel Air Beauville nine-passenger station wagon, purchased new in 1956 by the Casagrande family. "Luckily my Dad never parted with anything," Steve said. The Chevy was used to tow the yellow and white '59 Airflyte to Yosemite and beach towns around California.

Steve, wife Diane, and their family now use the Shasta to go camping. His children and grandchildren are making memories in a trailer that has now seen four generations of this family. Steve said it is about the grandkids and his desire for them to continue to enjoy the trailer and camping. As he said, "There is no better feeling than sitting at the table in a 1959 Shasta with the glow from the propane lantern."

Steve Casagrande and his 1959 Shasta trailer, towed by his parents' original 1956 Chevrolet Bel Air Beauville station wagon.

ABOVE: The Casagrande grandkids: Chloe, Dario, and Luca (back, left to right); Michael and Mathew (front, left to right). BELOW: The Casagrande brothers: Richard and Steve (back, left to right); Tom, Tim, and Gene (front, left to right).

Donna and Danny Myers

In 1953, Donna Myers' grandparents James and Pearl Rupard, and her parents, Don and Rusty Van Dame, pooled their funds and bought a new 1953 Aljoa for hunting trips and vacationing with the family. And so began many happy days of camping at Doheny and San Clemente state beaches in Southern California, along with side trips to the local mountains and Mexico.

As a young girl, Donna recalls her parents setting up cots for the kids in the outside cabana, a totally enclosed room off the trailer with tar-paper flooring. Her parents slept in the trailer. Donna said it didn't matter to the kids if they were outside, because all they did in camp was eat and sleep. Days were spent on the beach swimming, surfing, and fishing.

Donna's dad was happiest when he was outdoors fishing and hunting. Don

loved to swim, surf, fish, and dive for abalone in Mexico. He and Donna's grandfather also took the trailer to the local mountains to hunt for deer and quail and do some fishing in local lakes.

While searching through her mom's photo albums for pictures of the Aljoa, Donna noticed what a strong resemblance there was between her parents and Lucy and Desi Arnaz, well-known TV personalities in the 1950s and '60s. It's hard to tell in the black-and-white photos, but Don was very dark, with black hair, and Rusty was a fair redhead. It wasn't unusual for them to be stuck at the Mexican border answering questions about whether Donna's dad was a local or not.

All through the '50s and '60s, Donna's family spent many happy evenings

All photos on pages 168–69 submitted by Donna Myers.

around the campground barbecue, eating fish or abalone her dad had caught during the day. Days were spent floating in the ocean, catching waves on their canvas "surf riders," and building sand castles on the beach. Donna recalls her favorite time of day was when her dad finished fishing and would take her out in the surf in the late afternoon. "I always felt nothing could harm us while he held me and we jumped over the waves."

These great holidays lasted until 1967, when they took the Aljoa on its final trip to Mexico. Following that trip, the family took the trailer to Lake Elsinore and the property where her mom grew up. There the Aljoa sat and became a storage shed. Sometime after that a tree limb fell on the trailer, leaving one side severely damaged.

In the meantime, Donna had grown up, married a great guy named Danny, and raised two daughters. Along the way Donna and Danny fell in love with all things vintage, including vintage camper trailers, rallies, and the people they met there. Around 2005, Donna mentioned to Danny she would like to restore her family's Aljoa trailer still sitting in the pasture in Lake Elsinore. They looked at it but decided at that time it had too much damage from the fallen tree limb. They continued to look at other trailers but Donna kept coming back to the Aljoa, trying to convince Danny how much fun it would be to get her back on the road. Donna's mom thought they were crazy to think about spending money on the old "storage shed" trailer in the field. With the hobby becoming very popular and vintage trailers harder to find, Danny and Donna decided to take a closer look at the family trailer.

With the help of some trailer friends and a little encouragement from Donna, Danny decided that the Aljoa could be saved. The kitchen area had to be rebuilt. Kitchen cabinets on the damaged side had to be replaced,

along with most of the interior paneling. They were able to save the original floors and recover the click-clack seats in the front. The wood detail over the seating area had not been too damaged, but the table was missing. All the hardware was still on the cabinets and some of the original camping dishes were still in the cupboards. The original trailer did not have a bathroom, so they reconfigured the rear bedroom area so a toilet could be added. The

exterior was painted, doors were rehung, and the original screen doors were refinished.

Danny and Donna are in the process of returning to her family home, where the Aljoa first entered their life. The Aljoa is now sitting in the same space beside the family home that it occupied back in 1953. It continues to be the center of many great family memories.

The Glampers

If you are reading this book you are probably well aware of "glamping" (glamorous camping). These women are breaking all of the rules, blending lace with the great outdoors, and retrofitting vintage trailers (mostly from the 1960s and 1970s) with a style all their own. Each one is a unique expression of the glamper herself.

FACING: **The glamorous interior of Tabatha and Lexis Nothaft's 1988 Coleman Sun Valley pop-up (see page 197).**

Adam and Stacie Guzman

Adam and Stacie Guzman personalized their 1961 Field and Stream in just a few months. Starting with an original trailer in decent condition, Stacie put her feminine touch on the interior and Adam was allowed to take some more macho liberties with the outside. The inside wood was brightened up with off-white paint and lots of pillows and lace. No respectable glamper would be without a chandelier, which adds to the very girly interior. On the exterior, the diamond plate, a rear truck bumper, and new paint (with the original Field and Stream stripe) make this trailer the perfect blend of both styles for these trailerites' first (but not last) trailer.

Amanda Cocanougher

Amanda Cocanougher, a hairstylist and makeup artist, wanted a trailer to use on location in Nashville, Tennessee. Her parents, Sonny and Sherry Thompson, found her a 1965 Barth on Craigslist. The family spent nine months restoring "Rosie," named after Amanda's mother's middle name. Now, Rosie is used for bridal parties, birthday parties, photo shoots, and any special event that requires getting glamoured up!

All photos this page submitted by Amanda Cocanougher.

Vicki Taylor

All photos this page submitted by Vicki Taylor.

A vintage camper trailer enthusiast who was a friend of Vicki Taylor's shared with her the fun she was having while camping with Sisters on the Fly. Even though Vicki had never towed her own trailer before, the idea of camping with a bunch of ladies appealed to her and she started looking for a trailer. She found her 1957 Mercury almost five hours away and had her husband, Skip, tow it home so she could start decorating. Now Vicki enjoys glamping as a member of both Sisters on the Fly and Get'away Gals, camping groups for women only. She loves to camp with her two rescue poodles: a five-pound toy poodle named Sophie, represented by the tiny poodle on the side of the camper; and a fifty-five-pound standard poodle named Mila, who's also on the side of the camper. Vicki loves the outdoors and biking and hiking with her dogs. This city secretary continues to practice her towing and backing skills and is loving her time with her trailer "Tallulah."

Beth Bricker

Beth Bricker and her husband, Don, from Michigan, were enjoying a car show when Beth saw a display of vintage camper trailers. That Tin Can Tourists display led Beth on a hunt for her own trailer. With the help of her father, Ron Stamm, she found a Frolic at a yard sale for $150. It was so dilapidated that it required a ride home to Beth's house on the back of a flatbed trailer.

Undeterred by the negative comments from family and friends, Beth started planning her restoration. One friend had seen Beth's trailer and thought she had totally lost her marbles for considering restoring such a pile of garbage. So when her friend saw another Frolic at an auction in much better shape, she called Beth and offered to bid on it for her. Beth was so excited that she found her husband and hustled him out of the car show they were attending. Thankfully the friend won the auction for Beth, so she had a much better trailer to restore.

Don helped get the 1966 Frolic home, showed her how to use some tools, and encouraged her to do the restoration on the Frolic. Beth has worked at a lumberyard for years and didn't hesitate taking on the restoration. She redid the floor, added new trim, and replaced some rotten wood. Beth even found a wedding cake taillight being used as a reflector on a neighbor's tree. She bought it and now has matching taillights for her Frolic. The original Frolic was sold to a hunter to live out its life as a deer stand.

Beth is now Sister on the Fly No. 2987, as well as a member of the Tin Can Tourists and the Loyal Order of the Glamper. She takes the trailer out several times a year. Don is happy to join her, and they are enjoying the vintage trailer hobby together.

Photos on pages 178–79 submitted by Beth Bricker.

Chad and Elizabeth Cheely

Chad Cheely and his wife, Elizabeth, were inspired by the time they spent in Jekyll Island, Georgia, over the years. It was there that they fell in love, got engaged, married, and still continue to visit at least three times a year. While tent camping on the island on one of their excursions, the heat index reached 115 degrees. Chad thought, "There has to be a better way!"

After contemplating a few ideas on improving their camping situation, Chad and Elizabeth met a couple who restored vintage trailers. The couples became fast friends, and the Cheelys were inspired to own their own vintage camper trailer.

One day, following a failed attempt to purchase a trailer, the couple stopped by an antique store. The proprietor was asking about their day, and while they were telling her about their desire to purchase a vintage trailer, another customer overheard their conversation. She informed them that her neighbor had a trailer parked in the woods on her property and suggested they go by and see if she would be willing to sell. That's precisely what they did. The 1979 Nomad was in rough shape, and Chad initially talked himself out of buying the trailer. Later that night, while mulling it over with Elizabeth, they decided to purchase the trailer. The next day they drove home with their "new pile of garbage."

The restoration was a huge undertaking for Chad and Elizabeth and the several family members who volunteered to help. After stripping the entire thing down to the bones, they were able to start putting her back together. Once the new floors were down, the process got easier. Restoring the trailer to make sure it was roadworthy was a lot of work. Decorating was the fun part. Going back to their time and memories spent on the beach, they decided to decorate it in a retro beach style. "Goin' Coastal" has inspired the Cheely family to take a shot at restoring another camper very soon. They agree that "restoring these beauties is hard work but so rewarding in the end."

All photos on pages 180-81 by Chad C. Cheely.

Christy McVay

Both photos this page by Christy McVay.

After several e-mails and phone conversations, Christy McVay of Milner, Georgia, decided to drive six and a half hours to North Carolina to buy her 1971 Jayco Jay Wren. Christy and her dad, Bill Mann, had new tires put on the trailer and towed it back to Georgia, where Christy and her family helped get the Jay Wren all glamped out and ready to go to rallies.

The Jay Wren has been a family project. Christy's seventy-three-year-old mother, Carole Mann, hand-painted the outside of the trailer. The aluminum has a wood grain texture so the brushstrokes cannot be seen. Christy and her mother covered the cushions and made new curtains. They worked hard to keep the interior in the original 1970s décor of avocado, gold, and orange. In the summer, Christy does change it up a bit and exchanges her orange décor with blue to make it more summery. Much of the décor has come from Christy's family.

Recently celebrating her twenty-fifth year of employment as a loan closer at a local bank, Christy enjoys finding 1970s treasures at yard and estate sales. Christy's daughter, a budding artist, drew a caricature of her mother's trailer. After looking at her drawing, Christy decided to name her camper "Birdie." As a member of Southern Vintage Trailer Friends, she's attended several rallies and has grown to love these experiences. Christy is looking forward to more rallies with Birdie. "Hopefully it will be something that I will continue to do for many years to come."

Julie Flavin

Wanting to photograph Burning Man in 2010, wine distributor Julie Flavin found her 1967 Cardinal for sale in Portland, Oregon. It was red and white with a birch interior. It had "pretty good bones, but needed a bit of love." Julie was willing and able to supply the love. She decorated the trailer in disco lounge décor. She included a disco ball, lava lamp, leopard pillows, turquoise couches, and a wine rack and bar, which she had professionally painted turquoise and white. She added big flower decals, and on the back painted "Winebuff's Chick Shack" in bold letters. Julie then headed to Burning Man where the trailer did fantastic and was the hit of her campmates.

Now the trailer resides with Julie's good friend Jennifer Heberlien in Arizona. Jennifer travels all over with the Cardinal. Julie has since bought and sold a 1959 Airstream. She now has a completely restored 1967 Silver Streak. The Silver Streak will be her retirement trailer, as she continues to enjoy vintage camping.

All photos this page submitted by Julie Flavin.

All photos this page submitted by Natalie Owens.

Natalie Owens

Natalie Owens dreamed of owning her own trailer to have a "girly girl's place" in the world of boys in which she resides. She is a misplaced Texan living on a Kansas wheat farm, raising beef cattle and twin boys. Owning a glamper had always just been a bit of a dream until she attended a vintage junk show. There was a glamped-out trailer there selling hand-sewn textiles and Natalie was smitten. She spent more than three hours looking at the trailer and getting tips and encouragement from its owner on the possibilities of owning her own trailer. Natalie said she "knew in her soul it was time, and God handled the rest."

Natalie's camper, a 1969 Cardinal Deluxe, belonged to a friend's husband. The trailer had been in his family since his grandfather bought it brand new, and had been used by their family until it was parked in the back of a shed. It stayed in the shed with the exception of its yearly duty during hay-baling season, where it was parked in the field as a place for the workers to sleep. With a bit of coaxing, her friend's husband agreed to sell Natalie the Cardinal. When she finally took ownership of the trailer and had the chance to look inside, it took her breath away. It was in excellent condition. Natalie was so excited she couldn't sleep for days, as plans for the trailer kept her mind buzzing from idea to idea. The trailer is now used to take her boys for weekend camping trips, but its main use is a rolling boutique for Natalie's jewelry business she started in 1999.

Jill Henson

Jill Henson, a pharmaceutical representative from Fort Worth, Texas, wanted to use her six-week sabbatical to camp across the United States. Visiting each state is on Jill's bucket list. Preferring the shininess of the vintage Airstreams, Jill started her search for a trailer by looking online. After several months of searching, she found "the one." It was a twenty-two-foot 1959 Airstream Flying Cloud, which she named "Mabel." With much of the basic restoration already completed, Jill only had to do a bit of electrical work and then the decorating could begin. The interior of the trailer had already been painted, but she decided to paint it again to meet her ideas of how Mabel should look. "Mabel had to be all decked out in vintage cowgirl style."

Once she finished putting her touch on the trailer, Jill loaded up Mabel and her dogs and headed way out west. She visited eleven states and traveled almost ten thousand miles. Jill continues to take Mabel camping. She is looking forward to her next sabbatical, when she plans on getting closer to completing her goal of visiting each state in the nation.

All photos this page submitted by Jill Henson.

David and Julia Wilson

David and Julia Wilson from Danville, Illinois, have raised three children. They camped with their kids while they were growing up and loved it. Now their kids are grown and living in Wisconsin, Colorado, and Indiana. While perusing the Internet, Julia found articles and pictures of glampers that piqued her interest. The Wilsons started their search for a camper by looking at ads in the five states surrounding Illinois. Unfortunately the search was full of long drives ending in disappointments. Their son ended up finding their trailer, a 1962 Oasis, in their hometown. It looked like it had some good bones so the Wilsons bought it.

David and Julia did a complete restoration on the Oasis. David even manufactured a black water tank, and redid the electrical, plumbing, and subfloor. Julia sewed new curtains and an awning for the Oasis. They primed, painted, decorated, and enjoyed the process of restoring their trailer. Julia said the trailer has been "a labor of love."

They named their glamper "Lucy Mae," after their grandmothers, and are now enjoying camping in a glamper. Julia can read or scrapbook while David is fishing. The couple has found their old "Wilson" camper sign, and you can now see it hanging in their front window while the couple relaxes in Lucy Mae.

All photos this page submitted by David and Julia Wilson.

Maggie Banowetz

Sister on the Fly No. 2389 felt "Aunt Bea" speak to her the minute she stepped into her broken-down little 1956 Cal Craft. Maggie Banowetz of Santa Ana, California, and her husband, Roger, had been debating buying a vintage trailer or a new trailer for Maggie to tow behind her Subaru Forester. Maggie really wanted the feel of the old trailer with its wooden interior and vintage charm. Roger wasn't so keen on inheriting someone else's problems. After looking at a lot of trailers, Maggie said she felt like she and Aunt Bea were the perfect match. The only problem was convincing Roger. But in the end, even he succumbed to Aunt Bea's charm.

After purchasing the Cal Craft in 2010, Maggie spent the next three years working on her and getting her ready to shine. They worked with John Palmer to restore and repair her frame, while Roger did the electrical and plumbing repairs. Maggie hunted up vintage fabric and sewed curtains and pillows to gussy her up.

Now Maggie and Aunt Bea, decked out in her charming black, red, and white polka dots, are busy at Sister on the Fly events and rallying with fellow trailerites, happy to be together!

Renee Moore, Tricia Charles, and Peggy Coble

Photos (above and below) submitted by Renee Moore.

Renee Moore, an independent marketing associate, had been dreaming of owning a vintage trailer. She and her sister, insurance agent Tricia Charles, and their mother, retired hospice nurse Peggy Coble, had been collecting items for the trailer they one day would own. While enjoying their big toy hauler trailers, they wanted a glamper for "girl time." Renee even made sure her last vehicle came with a tow package—"just in case."

Casually looking for a trailer, Renee found a 1974 Caveman for sale on Craigslist. Following a family discussion, Peggy decided that if the trailer met their needs (and wasn't another project for the men in their lives to work on), she would buy and gift the trailer to her girls. The John Deere Yellow trailer with its buttercup interior was a perfect fit for the ladies, and they towed her home. They named her "Miss Lulubug" after Peggy's childhood trailer and the *Little Lulu* cartoon. Together, this mom and daughter team have painted, sewn, decorated, and shopped to outfit Miss Lulubug. They have attended their first rally and plan on making many more memories as they share the joys of camping together.

Shayna and Rick West

Shayna and Rick West from Springfield, Missouri, met in 2005 while sport skydiving. In October 2005, Shayna had a tragic skydiving accident when both of her parachutes failed to function properly. She ended up landing face first on a blacktop parking lot at an estimated fifty miles per hour. When Shayna and Rick got to the hospital, they learned she was two weeks pregnant with their son, Tanner. He was born in June 2006, and is completely unaffected by Shayna's accident and subsequent surgeries and medications. Prior to having kids, the Wests' lives revolved around skydiving. Once kids came into the picture, they knew they needed a new hobby, and vintage camping became that for their family.

Not afraid of taking a road trip to find the perfect trailer, Shayna went online and found "Petunia" for sale in Colorado. When she called the number, she found out the ad was an old listing and Petunia had been sold months ago. Shayna started searching again the next morning. She looked everywhere and then Petunia's picture popped up for sale in Rockport, Texas. Shayna quickly called and was first on the list to come and take a look. The West family, now including their daughter, Bridget, set off on their sixteen-hour drive to meet Petunia. It turned out that the woman who had purchased the trailer in Colorado had taken Petunia on a two-week road trip, and was now passing her on to a new

family. Shayna and her family felt it was the trailer they were meant to have. They happily hitched her up and set off for Missouri. They ended up having their first (unscheduled) campout in Petunia along historic Route 66 due to truck trouble. The next day they were able to make it home despite a large snowstorm.

Following her skydiving accident, Shayna was diagnosed with post-traumatic stress disorder. She always tells people that Petunia is her happy place. Priceless memories are being made, and the West family looks forward to making many, many more.

All photos on pages 190-91 submitted by Shayna and Rick West.

Shirley and Patrick Rossetti

Shirley Rossetti's uncle purchased a 1968 Prowler from the original owner in the early '70s and owned and loved it for thirty years. Shirley remembers her aunt and uncle and their four kids bringing it to the annual family campout every year. Over the years her uncle added insulation, an air conditioner, and a microwave. Shirley's aunt had kept the upholstery covered most of those years, keeping it in really good condition.

In 2009, Shirley and her husband, Patrick, bought the Prowler in basically great condition. The corner of the back bathroom had a leak and some rot. During the teardown of the back end of the trailer and the subsequent repair, they decided to take the shower out and replace it with much-needed storage shelves. Patrick, with the help of Shirley's brother, used pressure-treated wood for the studs and replumbed the shower to the outside so that they now have warm water to rinse sandy feet, fill large pots for cooking, and other things.

The Rossettis weren't looking for a vintage camper; they just wanted something used and inexpensive to take their four kids out for fun. Shirley took one look at the avocado green, burnt orange, and harvest yellow décor, green appliances, and mushroom decorations and thought, "Eeks, what can I do with this?!" About that time, they joined the Oregon chapter of Rollin' Oldies Vintage Trailers, and the group encouraged them to keep the original

All photos on pages 192-93 submitted by Shirley and Patrick Rossetti.

upholstery and redecorate around those colors. Shirley made new curtains, matching pillows, a pennant banner, and found some retro mushroom decorations on eBay.

Whether Shirley and Patrick are camping with extended family at their parish campout, the gals of International Glamping Weekend, or just Shirley's little family, they always end up having a good time and making some great memories.

Sonia Young

Sonia Young loves to collect vintage. Following her move back to California in 2010, she was looking for a way to find friends and create a community of people around her. After perusing the Internet, she found a group of ladies that were camping together in vintage camper trailers. She thought that looked like fun. Camping, towing, and trailering had never crossed Sonia's mind before, but after thinking about it a bit, she decided to look into it further. Sonia was excited to take on a new challenge and try something she had never done.

Sonia was born a "congenital amputee" of all four limbs—a rare condition. She's conquered many challenges in her lifetime. When she was two, doctors suggested her parents have Sonia's legs amputated so she could hopefully walk with prosthetics. This decision was not a flippant one, as the chances of success were only fifty-fifty. Her parents were given two years to decide. Sonia recalls her mom telling her that she spent hours, months, and years in prayer, even bartering with God for Sonia's recovery before they went ahead with the amputation. The surgery was successful, and at four years old, Sonia got her first pair of prosthetic legs.

She recalls being so excited about choosing her shiny black leather Mary Janes. Sonia recalls her mother telling her, "As soon as you tried on your first little legs, you took to them as if they were your real legs!"

Against all odds, Sonia never slowed down. She has had dozens of prosthetics over her lifetime. Sonia is very excited to now have her prosthetics being custom-made by Hanger Clinic, the same company who made the dolphin's prosthetic tail in the movie *Dolphin Tale*.

Sonia was born in Santa Barbara, California, and has lived in Alaska, Massachusetts, and California. Approaching her fortieth birthday, she decided she needed a change of scenery and moved to Alaska sight unseen, taking her two youngest children with her. She didn't tell her family until a few days before her move because she didn't want to hear all the reasons why she shouldn't go. After seven years in Alaska, she again decided to move to a new place. This time Sonia visited the East Coast and chose western Massachusetts before moving there.

At the urging of her eldest son, she moved back to California in 2010 to

All photos on pages 194-96 by Jason B. Lee.

care for her father as he was passing away. Sonia's father was her greatest supporter. When Sonia was born, the doctors came into the recovery room and asked her parents, "Do you accept this child or do you want to institutionalize her?" Sonia's mother told her that her dad looked those doctors in the eyes and without a moment's hesitation said, "Of course I want her—she's my daughter!"

After spending a few years dealing with the loss of her father and surgeries she needed, Sonia decided to seriously pursue finding a vintage trailer. She looked at several trailers but they just didn't click with her sense of vintage. Then she spotted a 1956 Jewel for sale online. She spoke to the seller and found out that the original owners had taken the Jewel on their dream trip to Alaska in 1956, the year her parents were married. Sonia felt like it was meant to be. She bought the trailer.

As soon as the seller delivered the Jewel to Sonia's home, she got to work making it her own. She decorated the interior using only authentic 1950s materials. Sonia loved the diamond window and the original birchwood of her trailer. She didn't mind the dings and scratches, as they reminded her that, much like herself, her Jewel had lived a lot of life and had the "beauty marks" to show for it.

Sonia removed the hideous brown carpet and replaced the flooring of her Jewel all by herself. As she was laying the glue down on the floor she just couldn't get the grip she needed on the trowel. She finally discarded the trowel and used her bare hands to lay the glue. It worked, and Sonia had successfully met another challenge with a creative solution.

Deciding to enter the world of vintage camper trailering had its rough spots, as some thought Sonia wouldn't be able to do the hobby on her own. Sonia proved them wrong and is now towing her Jewel around like a pro. She loves to camp in "Time Traveler" and hear the rainfall on the aluminum. Sonia is excited to meet new friends and travel to new places. She is more than willing to educate people on her disability, but appreciates when people look at her as a person and do not define her by what they perceive she is able or unable to accomplish. She is a natural at advocating for anyone with a disability. Sonia's dad would be so happy to see that his legacy of hope, courage, and acceptance is bringing such joy and accomplishment to Sonia's life as well as others.

Tabatha and Lexis Nothaft

Desiring to share a camping experience with her seventeen-year-old daughter, Lexis, Tabatha Nothaft searched for a small camper trailer on the Internet. Tabatha said that glamper trailers kept popping up and each one was so unique that it inspired her to buy and glamp out her own vintage trailer.

Tabatha and Lexis started their glamping experience with a 1965 Serro Scotty HiLander. After completing that trailer, Tabatha had the fever for glamping and was ready for another project. Looking for something a bit bigger and more unique, Tabatha found a 1988 Coleman Sun Valley pop-up. In just

Photos below submitted by Tabatha and Lexis Nothaft.

six weeks, Lexis and Tabatha were able to completely glamp out their newest trailer. Watching how-to videos and tackling the trailer together was an awesome mother-daughter bonding experience. Lexis loves her "dollhouse trailer."

Lexis and Tabatha glamp in the backyard and at campgrounds almost every weekend near their home in the Hamptons. They are looking forward to taking longer excursions with their trailers, exploring new territory and meeting new friends. With their pink trailer, it's hard for people not to notice this incredible mother-daughter team.

Lisa Long, Patty Spence, and Debbie Daw

Three women happened to attend the same home show in 2012 where there were vintage camper trailers displayed by Sisters on the Fly. The three all fell in love with the vintage trailers. Debbie Dow, Lisa Long, and Patty Spence, with their husbands' help, acquired vintage campers and started restoring and camping.

Lisa and Wade Long's 1966 Kit Companion.

Lisa and Wade Long went to the home show as owners of a '66 Kit Companion. What they saw at the show spurred on their creativity and desire to be part of the vintage camper trailer hobby. Together, this couple sketched and dreamed about how they wanted their trailer to look one day. They took their Kit Companion from flat black and camo to a striking red and white café-themed dollhouse. They did all the work themselves. Wade has found four more trailers by driving around, knocking on doors, and convincing the owners to sell. At this moment these trailers all need a bit of TLC from Lisa and Wade. This couple has no trouble dreaming about how they are going to restore the next trailer. As natural junkers, they love to find the treasures needed to accessorize their newest project.

After attending the home show in 2012, Patty Spence started collecting treasures to decorate a vintage camper trailer. The only problem was the stuff was adding up too quickly and she didn't yet have a trailer to put it all in. Soon her husband, Don Haley, said they had to get a trailer or a storage unit. In the early hours one morning, Patty found her

Patty Spence's 1965 Aloha reflects her cowgirl background.

'65 Aloha for sale on the Internet. She called the man selling the trailer and bought it sight unseen. It had been used as a hunter's shack and was quite dirty, but fortunately had very little rot. They were able to clean up the trailer and replace the wood ceiling and the stove. Don was able to reclaim his bedroom after Patty decorated her trailer in true cowgirl style. As a former barrel racer and lifelong cowgirl, the theme was a natural for Patty. She came up with the ideas and Don made them happen. What a team!

Debbie and Glen Dow looked and looked for a trailer. Debbie found one on Craigslist and went to have a look. Desperation mixed with desire allowed her to purchase their 1960 Oasis trailer. It was a complete mess and required extensive restoration. Not only did the Dows restore their trailer and start camping with fellow vintage trailerites, they started hosting a rally at their home as well! For the past three years, Debbie has invited thirty-five of her closest glamping friends to spend the weekend in her backyard.

They enjoy antiquing, potlucking, crafting, and camping. Glenn is the superhero of the weekend; along with his chores of setting up tables and chairs, he is on call to help the women out with the little things that need fixing while camping. Rumor has it that Glenn and Debbie host a wonderful campout.

Glenn Dow has always been a painter. Now that vintage camper trailers are part of his life, the trailers are finding their way into many of his beautiful landscapes. Vintage camper trailers have a tendency to do that—creep into every aspect of your life.

These three ladies and their husbands did not know each other just three short years ago. They are now fast friends and camp together quite often. It's amazing to see how trailers bring us together.